'This book reminds us that leadersh[ip]
Rich in humanity and insight, it's a n[...]
with purpose.'

— Chris W[...]

'A deeply authentic, thought-provoking and intensely practical book that challenges, provokes and ultimately empowers those committed to meaningful leadership.'

— Chris Badger, Care Quality Commission's (CQC's) new Chief Inspector of Adult Social Care and Integrated Care

'In a world that still undervalues Black voices, navigating your own path as a Black leader is an act of extraordinary courage and sacrifice that requires ongoing self-care. This book is both insightful and inspiring and I highly recommend it to all current and aspiring leaders.'

— Charles Kwaku-Odoi, Chief Executive, Caribbean and African Health Network (CAHN)

'Leaders often forget the importance of continuing their own learning, but this book is so compelling, insightful and extremely accessible that it draws the reader in. This is truly an excellent book, and I highly recommended it.'

— Professor Jane Harrington, Vice Chancellor and CEO, University of Greenwich

'This book demonstrates that the journey toward human leadership is not defined by easy choices or quick wins, but by experience, relationships, support, passion, public service and the desire to uplift those around us.'

— Professor Vic Rayner OBE, CEO, National Care Forum

'This book brings the road to leadership vividly to life and powerfully demonstrates what good leadership can achieve. A truly excellent read!'

— Nadra Ahmed CBE, Executive Chairman, the National Care Association.

'This powerful collection of leadership journeys offers authentic reflections, offers hopefulness and highlights the power of relationships and learning from each other. A truly must-read book.'

— Kenny Gibson, Deputy Director, NHS Safeguarding

'A compelling and thoughtful read for anyone interested in truly human-centred leadership. A highly accessible mix of contributions from experienced leaders and reflections on theory and practice.'

— Sarah McClinton, Chief Social Worker (Adults)

HUMAN LEADERSHIP

How to succeed (and how to fail) in the helping professions

Edited by Claudia Megele and Tanya Moore

Jessica Kingsley Publishers
London and Philadelphia

First published in Great Britain in 2026 by Jessica Kingsley Publishers
An imprint of John Murray Press

1

Copyright © Claudia Megele and Tanya Moore 2026

The right of Claudia Megele and Tanya Moore to be identified as the Author of the Work has been asserted by them in accordance with the Copyright, Designs and Patents Act 1988.

Chapter 1 © Anthony Douglas, Chapter 2 © Peter Buzzi and Claudia Megele, Chapter 3 © Tanya Moore, Chapter 4 © Anna Korving, Chapter 5 © Bill Mumford, Chapter 6 © Michael Sanders and Vanessa Hirneis, Chapter 7 © Peter Buzzi and Claudia Megele, Chapter 8 © Petros Oratis, Chapter 9 © Val Parker, Chapter 10 © Christopher Scanlon and John Adlam, Chapter 11 © Jim McManus, Chapter 12 © Clenton Farquharson, Chapter 13 © David Shemmings, Chapter 14 © Yvette Stanley, Chapter 15 © Michael Preston-Shoot, Chapter 16 © Godfred Boahen and Sarah Range, Chapter 17 © Sharon Shoesmith, Chapter 18 © Cedi Frederick

Figure 11.1 reproduced with permission from Wiggins and Smallwood, 2018.

All rights reserved. No part of this publication may be reproduced, stored in a retrieval system, or transmitted, in any form or by any means without the prior written permission of the publisher, nor be otherwise circulated in any form of binding or cover other than that in which it is published and without a similar condition being imposed on the subsequent purchaser.

A CIP catalogue record for this title is available from the
British Library and the Library of Congress

ISBN 978 1 80501 271 9
eISBN 978 1 80501 272 6

Printed and bound in Great Britain by CPI Group

Jessica Kingsley Publishers' policy is to use papers that are natural, renewable and recyclable products and made from wood grown in sustainable forests. The logging and manufacturing processes are expected to conform to the environmental regulations of the country of origin.

Jessica Kingsley Publishers
Carmelite House
50 Victoria Embankment
London EC4Y 0DZ

www.jkp.com

John Murray Press
Part of Hodder & Stoughton Ltd
An Hachette Company

The authorised representative in the EEA is Hachette Ireland, 8 Castlecourt Centre, Dublin 15, D15 XTP3, Ireland (email: info@hbgi.ie)

Contents

INTRODUCTION 7

Chapter 1. Leadership and Pressure 11
Anthony Douglas

Chapter 2. Leadership and Vulnerability 22
Peter Buzzi and Claudia Megele

Chapter 3. Leading Complexity 33
Tanya Moore

Chapter 4. Using Communication to Lead Change 43
Anna Korving

Chapter 5. Success, Failure and the Toll of Leadership 51
Bill Mumford

Chapter 6. Social Influence and Butterfly Effects 59
Michael Sanders and Vanessa Hirneis

Chapter 7. Emotional Culture and Leadership: Thinking about Emotions, Fear and Anxiety in the Workplace 71
Peter Buzzi and Claudia Megele

Chapter 8. Lateral Leadership: Authority and Influence Beyond the Hierarchy 82
Petros Oratis

Chapter 9. Sibling Leadership: Stepping Away from the Role of Overbearing Parent 91
Val Parker

Chapter 10. The Disappointed and the Disappointing: Learning for and about Leadership 101
Christopher Scanlon and John Adlam

Chapter 11. Relational Leadership in a Crisis 110
Jim McManus

Chapter 12. How to Build Co-Production: Involving People as Real Partners: Don't Wait to Put Your Ducks in a Row 119
Clenton Farquharson

Chapter 13. Supporting Practitioners Working with Uncertainty, Complexity and Risk: It *is* Rocket Science! 130
David Shemmings

Chapter 14. Authentic Leadership 137
Yvette Stanley

Chapter 15. Leadership Literacy: Reflections on Relational Leadership. 142
Michael Preston-Shoot

Chapter 16. Leadership for Environmental Sustainability 152
Godfred Boahen and Sarah Range

Chapter 17. Leadership and Blame. 162
Sharon Shoesmith

Chapter 18. Navigate Your Own Path to Leadership 173
Cedi Frederick

SUBJECT INDEX 181

AUTHOR INDEX 186

Introduction

When we think of successful leaders, images of confident, poised individuals commanding the room often come to mind. These leaders are celebrated for their achievements, lauded for their decisions and admired for their vision.

But what's often overlooked is the arduous journey and multitude of struggles that pave the way to their apparent success. Leadership is not merely a role to be assumed; it's a complex challenge that demands resilience, perseverance and a constant battle against a plethora of obstacles.

Stories of successful leaders often highlight their triumphs whilst glossing over the difficulties encountered along the way. Such selective narratives can create the illusion that leadership is inherently linked to success. They downplay the intense effort and numerous setbacks involved.

The late Steve Jobs is widely remembered for his role in revolutionizing the tech industry with Apple. But his journey was far from smooth, and he faced significant challenges, including being ousted in a very public way from the company he co-founded. His return to Apple and his subsequent success were the result of years of relentless work, innovation and learning from past failures. Yet the focus on his eventual success often eclipses the narrative of his years as a struggling and resilient leader.

Behind the veneer of successful leadership lies a trail of personal sacrifices. Leaders invest time, energy and self into their roles, often at the expense of their personal lives. The pressure to consistently perform and make pivotal decisions can lead to immense stress and burnout.

The popular idea of 'The Heroic Leader' as a lone figure who stands out from the crowd makes the journey of leadership a lonely one. In this book, we outline how good leadership in practice is instead about *connectedness*. Connected leaders harness the power of relationships and belongingness to enhance creativity, growth and development and to achieve great results.

But the responsibility that comes with making high-stakes decisions can create a sense of separation from others and evoke feelings of loneliness. This can be further aggravated by the myths that leaders must be 'strong' and that admitting any vulnerability undermines one's authority. These traditional ideas can place pressure on leaders to maintain a façade of confidence and infallibility – an expectation that it's *their* responsibility to inspire and guide *others*.

This in turn promotes a culture in which showing doubt or seeking help is perceived as weakness. Such a culture can be isolating and lead to significant challenges as leaders struggle with the weight of their responsibilities in solitude.

Vulnerability is often perceived as a weakness, especially in the realm of leadership where strength, decisiveness and confidence are traditionally valued. Increasingly, however, there's recognition of the *power of vulnerability* in leadership. Vulnerability can be shown through a willingness to openly express emotions, admit mistakes and acknowledge uncertainties. It involves being authentic and transparent, and allowing our true self to be seen and understood by others. Such openness can break down barriers, build trust and create a safe space for others to express themselves, fostering a culture of honesty and collaboration. In this book, you will read about how embracing vulnerability can lead to stronger connections, enhanced trust and greater authenticity. Ultimately, it can foster a more resilient and effective organizational culture. (See 'Vulnerability and emotionally exposed leadership' in Chapter 2 of this book.)

Jacinda Ardern, the previous Prime Minister of New Zealand, has been widely praised for her empathetic leadership style, particularly in her handling of crises such as the Christchurch mosque shootings and the Covid-19 pandemic. On 15 March 2019, a white supremacist carried out an attack on Christchurch mosque, killing 51 people. Ardern immediately responded with deep empathy, visiting the victims' families, wearing hijab as a sign of respect and openly grieving with the Muslim community.

Ardern's approach highlights the importance of emotions in leadership, demonstrating that vulnerability, empathy and understanding are integral to leading effectively, especially in times of crisis. Her emotional leadership, empathy and clear and unequivocal message of unity and solidarity set an example for leaders across the world.

Ardern's effective emotional leadership and empathetic communication became two of the defining features of her leadership that proved to be particularly important and impactful during the Covid-19 pandemic.

During the pandemic, she regularly addressed the nation with calmness and clarity, often from her own home, which made her appear more relatable and accessible. Her use of social media, particularly Facebook Live sessions, allowed her to connect directly with New Zealanders, answering their questions and addressing their concerns in real time. This approach helped to build trust and ensure compliance with strict lockdown measures, which were among the most effective in the world.

Ardern's approach highlights the importance of the Emotional Leader, who demonstrates that vulnerability, empathy and understanding are integral to leading effectively, especially in times of crisis.

Similarly, Satya Nadella, the CEO of Microsoft, is an example of empathy, vulnerability and emotional leadership in the corporate world. After joining Microsoft, Nadella introduced the concept of 'growth mindset' to Microsoft, encouraging employees to learn from failure, seek feedback and continuously develop their skills. Nadella often speaks about the impact of his personal experiences on his leadership style, particularly the influence of his son's disability. His openness about the challenges his family has faced has made him a more empathetic and understanding leader. This vulnerability has helped him connect with employees on a deeper level and transform the culture, business strategy and fortunes of Microsoft.

This leadership style is increasingly recognized for its ability to create inclusive, collaborative and resilient organizations through its values of empathy, communication and mutual respect.

You might think that, as individuals in organizations whose core business is people, leaders in health, social care, education, the public sector and the voluntary sector would practise relational leadership as a default position.

But this isn't a given. Environmental factors play a big part; for example, sustained funding and recruitment pressures of health and social care services over recent decades in the UK have created a state of near constant crisis in these sectors. It's at these most pressurized times, in 'survival mode', that leaders can default to the position of the Hierarchical and Controlling Leader.

In this book, emotionally exposed relational leaders and researchers share their failures and successes with you to offer compelling insights and strategies, and valuable lessons for us all – from managers involved in direct practice to CEOs. Their stories highlight the inevitable challenges as well as the power and impact of emotionally exposed leadership.

These chapters will show you how vulnerability, relational ability, social capital, empathy and effective communication and emotional capabilities can help you to navigate the complex and demanding landscape of the contemporary workplace.

To aid learning, each chapter of the book ends with some questions for you to consider in relation to your own leadership journey.

• Chapter 1 •

LEADERSHIP AND PRESSURE

Anthony Douglas

> Anthony Douglas CBE spent 26 years as Chief Executive of Cafcass. He is currently developing the National Practice Framework in Wales and is the Independent Chair of the Suffolk Safeguarding Partnership.
>
> Anthony has been a government adviser on a range of reviews and programmes, including: youth crime; a review of the Crown Prosecution Service for the Cabinet Office (2008); Foreign and Commonwealth Office reviews of child and adult safeguarding on St Helena (2018), Turks and Caicos (2018), Cayman Islands, Anguilla and Montserrat (2019), and Bermuda (2021, continuing); and is Department for Education Children's Commissioner in North East Lincolnshire (continuing).

I was chief executive of Cafcass – an organization that provides independent advice to the family courts about what is safe for children and in their best interest – between 2004 and 2019.

Cafcass was founded on 1 April 2001 as part of the UK Government's commitment to create greater consistency in the social work provided for UK family courts.

I'd estimate conservatively that my unforced labour over that 15-year span amounts to about 45,000 hours, holding 14,000 meetings, engaging in over a million conversations and writing over 3 million words – mostly dispensable emails. During that time, Cafcass supported 1.5 million children and young people throughout England and Wales.

Until 2010, Cafcass was repeatedly judged as inadequate by Ofsted. It had huge operational backlogs and thousands of children's cases remaining unallocated, but somehow, during my years as chief executive, I managed to convince politicians and my own board that I knew what I was doing. Eventually, we were judged as outstanding in 2018 – a rating that has been maintained ever since.

When I was tasked by the Cabinet Office with reviewing the Crown Prosecution Service as a government adviser in 2008, the Director of Public Prosecutions at the time, Keir Starmer, asked me not to be too harsh on them, as they were still a young organization and only 25 years old; Cafcass was founded in 2001, so at the time of writing is now 24 years old.

In this chapter, I reflect upon my experiences as chief executive of Cafcass and have structured the chapter to follow a sequential timeline that highlights how the organization and my leadership changed over time, plus the key lessons I've learnt along the way. You'll note that at times there is an overlap with the timeline and different lessons learnt. This is intentional given that learning and reflection aren't always linear.

When and where did it all start? (2004)

I was working in Suffolk, extremely happily, when I took a call that changed my life. It was from a friend of a friend suggesting I apply to run Cafcass, which was in deep trouble at the time.

I learnt eventually that the key to success is to have a team of highly competent people in place with no weak links, with everyone understanding their role and being committed to the overall objective. If those people are in place and come to work every day, success will follow as sure as night follows day.

But to begin with, I didn't have any of them, despite many of those early colleagues working night and day to keep the show on the road, regardless of how desperate the situation was. The heroic and battered workforces of failing organizations should never be taken for granted.

Learning from the early days (2004–2006)

Although the idea of Cafcass attracted widespread support, the reality in those first few years attracted mass disenchantment.

Poor appointments of senior managers and board members were made, and no organization can flourish without strong and capable leaders, be it a national government or a start-up.

Integrating 117 local and national organizations into a single national culture without a transition plan or a Theory of Change was impossible; there was no plan describing or illustrating what changes were needed and why, how these changes were going to take place and how they were going to achieve the organizational objectives or desired outcomes. Without such clarity, the mission was doomed from the start. Systems were non-existent, which meant that staff and contractors were free to do what they liked.

A lesson for government is that civil servants without relevant operational experience should never be allowed to run an operational service. When I started, the work itself was largely invisible. The early national management team was comprised of a single head of operations and eight directors of corporate services, including three directors of law. In combination, this created a corporate structure heavily skewed towards the administrative and legal aspects of the work rather than its core business operation, which was that of representing the best interests of children and families.

It took me several restructures to put in place an operational structure that positioned the work – and children and young people – at the heart of Cafcass so that we were a children's service in court and not an administrative court service.

Only then did the thousands of unallocated cases – unallocated children and young people – begin to steadily be allocated. Only then did the 'experiment of Cafcass' start to make sense.

Surviving (2004–2011)

My first few years were a test of survival. Not survival of the fittest, as I was drinking far too much red wine for that.

I drew upon my own personal adverse childhood experiences to develop an even tougher external shell. We received one inadequate inspection report after another, yet somehow, I managed to convince government ministers and senior civil servants that I was still the best person for the job. I expect that now, in today's more aggressive performance culture, I would have been sacked by 2008 at the latest.

But when I told sceptics that I was the best person to turn the situation around because I had slowly come to know and grasp the organization, its people and its cultures, I was speaking the truth.

And slowly I found some amazing people to come and work for me. I looked for mavericks and entrepreneurs. I needed people who could look at a problem, think differently about it and do whatever was needed to sort it.

By 2006, Cafcass had an amazing board run by two peers of the realm with relevant experience and the requisite backbone. A series of small successes began to add up to something big.

I had survived and so had the organization, and children and young people were getting a better deal.

Starting to get it right: building the team and culture (2010 onwards)

Our improvement journey had some clear phases and milestones, yet the timeline was never linear. Some things got better; other things got worse. I'd liken it to putting out a fire that is still in flames – even after extinguishing a flare-up, it can quickly grow again if left unchecked, as embers are never quite extinguished.

This was especially true between 2007 and 2010. I learnt how to use task forces to 'wrap around' a problem, whether the 'new flare-up' was 2000 unanswered complaints or tackling unallocated cases in far-flung corners of the country.

In the case of the unallocated cases, relocating employees from one geographical area to another naturally had a significant impact on their lives and families and therefore needed to be done in consultation and agreement with the people concerned. At that time, I had some amazing practice managers who would, without notice, take themselves off to live in another part of the country for a few weeks or months to troubleshoot. Mobilizing staff is not always easy, and I have seen a number of national organizations that never mobilize the potential they have within their workforce to solve problems in other parts of the same organization; so it was impressive to see managers relocate on their own initiative for weeks and months to address issues and overcome difficulties in different parts of their service.

By 2010, we had in place a talent management programme, which eventually had more than 200 staff enrolled. The criterion for acceptance to the programme was showing the ability to jump two levels of a professional hierarchy beyond their current role. Staff were nominated by their managers as part of the supervision and performance management process.

The main lesson I learnt from this time was that you can struggle with a problem for years. But if you get the right person in charge of sorting it, and if you give them a solid team, it can improve in weeks – a little like how some children start to thrive in foster care within a few days having been neglected for years.

The other lesson I learnt was that the only way to create sufficient power and traction to unite a large national workforce is to ensure clarity of goals and values. In the case of Cafcass, these goals and values are compelling – protecting the rights and best interests of children and young people, and for this work to be done well.

It was as simple and as complicated as that.

Children and young people's role in the Cafcass improvement journey (2006 and throughout)

Starting in 2006, we began to engage with a number of children and young people who had experience of the care system or whose futures were often being scarred for life in bitterly contested private law cases. Their cases were active, and they gladly gave us a running commentary of their experience, as they just wanted help. This gave the senior leaders a better understanding of young people's experiences, and listening to their voices and wishes contributed to shaping and improving the service. It was the first time as a senior leader that I understood how the lived experience of people who use services can help to shape how those services are designed and delivered.

This experience also helped me get back in touch with the reason I went into social work in the first place – something that can at times become diluted or obliterated after years in management roles.

Another advantage of engaging more with children and young people was that I came to know some of the children and young people over a period of more than ten years. Some of their journeys through childhood were complex, traumatic and moving. While not comparable, in some ways there were parallels with the development of Cafcass.

A 15-year-old in despair after incredible trauma and in dispute with his local authority for alleged corporate neglect, who by 22 had been through university and started his own IT company, which was – and still is – doing well.

Two six-year-olds who stood up on a box behind a microphone and told their story of being weaponized in a divorce battle to a spellbound audience of 400 professionals at our second annual 'Voice of the Child' conference.

The current Family Justice Young People's Board (FJYPB) emerged from these chaotic, countercultural and mesmerizing beginnings. Today's FJYPB is composed of care-experienced young people and children with experience of private law cases between the ages of 7 and 25, and plays an important role in informing and supporting developments in the Family Justice System.

Young people met and influenced ministers and other government stakeholders, and during this time, I learnt the important role of influencers: people who could influence decisions or the decision-making process. Developing a strong narrative in team rooms about how we could best help children was instrumental in making our culture explicit and embedding our values in practice, but it was equally important that external influencers and stakeholders could understand and appreciate the organization's vision and journey.

I became the public face of Cafcass and used all the opportunities I had to convey the messages about the way we were continuously aiming to have a positive impact on children, young people and their families. I also used sound bites publicly, some of which caught on, like 'every day matters' for a child.

Now when I work with a system, I am courteous with hierarchies but I search out the influencers to work with.

Absorbing hostility (2004–2013)

Some disgruntled former staff attacked me for years, mainly via informal channels and through gossip. This would be far worse nowadays with more invasive and pervasive social media. Whilst it was unpleasant, I knew I had done the right thing moving them on and that the criticisms, such as dumbing the organization down, were naïve.

We had to allocate all cases, reduce the budget and improve quality simultaneously. This could only be done through changing the operational model to one based on 'proportionate working'. Working proportionately meant using resources wisely, so they were directed to children in greatest need and where we could make the largest positive impact.

Opposition politicians over the period of 2007–2009 were calling for the abolition of Cafcass. I had several stormy meetings with leading politicians and quite a few interrogations on the Today programme asking me to consider my position.

Fathers' groups hated me, seeing me as one of the main reasons that family courts were denying fathers access to and care of their children in bitterly contested private law disputes – even though I had only pointed out the damaging effect of domestic violence on children.

At times, such hostility extended to criminal behaviour to make a point. *Human faeces* were pushed through our office doors.

I learnt that all parties in a dispute may have a compelling case, but what matters is the impact of adult behaviour on children. So our practice model gradually evolved to focus more on child impact – to see a chronology as the child's chronology, not just the professional's incident-based chronology, and the timescale for a case referencing as the child's timescale, not just the court or agency timescale.

In 2011, I reached a rapprochement of sorts with the activists. Most disputes are resolved eventually but often so much time is wasted by starting at the beginning rather than the end. I met with the leading activists one Saturday morning in a remote farmhouse on the Welsh border. I had no guarantees that going there would not result in a wild stunt to generate more publicity, but it didn't, and we had a good session. Interestingly, the only other outsider present was a journalist from *The New York Times*.

Officialdom could learn a lot from the stagecraft of campaigners, which often makes business and government comms functions look wooden by comparison.

The other reason relations improved was that I agreed with a lot that the activists said about the pernicious impact on children of parental alienation – when, due to manipulation or false information by one parent, a child refuses to have a relationship with the other parent. Nothing as frequent and violent as domestic abuse and coercive control, but still real and corrosive.

Demand, cost and quality (2010–2014)

The demand for Cafcass's service rose exponentially in the years after 2009 following the traumatic death of Peter Connelly (referred to as 'Baby P' at the time) at the hands of his mother and her partner. Peter Connelly suffered more than 50 injuries over a period of eight months, during which he was seen multiple times by various professionals including doctors, nurses and social workers. This led to widespread public outrage and a media frenzy accusing social workers of lack of action, and resulted in a culture of fear and tangible hatred.

In turn, the unprecedented publicity and public outrage with social workers led to a rash of defensive practice. Understandably and mostly defensively, more children were taken into care in the years after the killing of Peter Connelly, a trend that is still rising now for a more complex set of reasons, including the long tail of Covid-19.

Such tragedies are often followed by a quintessentially British phenomenon. The official response to mistakes has often been to introduce additional checks and balances. When this is done, the net impact is that there are now several times the number of people watching the work as there are doing it. It was this reactive public policy that led to the creation of the Children's Guardian role in law, after Maria Colwell, a nine-year-old girl, was returned home from care without an adequate risk assessment only to be killed by her stepfather in 1974.

Between 2010 and 2014, the Cafcass caseload doubled from 70,000 cases a year to 140,000, while its budget was reduced by 15%, and we still needed to improve the quality of our work to satisfy Ofsted. Learning how to do this was my biggest achievement in my 15-year tenure.

I had to ensure that the whole organization understood the significance of our work and everyone realized that a single unallocated case was a violation of that child's rights.

Staff took on double or treble the work to keep to this standard. I learnt a lot about the wisdom of crowds – that if you can persuade an entire organization to work differently, you can change a culture and do what is needed.

Another major external impact was the reduced access to legal aid due to progressive cuts in the legal aid budget beginning in 2010. This meant that in private law cases of divorce and parental separation, many parents could not access legal aid and had to represent themselves, so the number of litigants in person rocketed. Cafcass practitioners and judges found themselves needing to help people navigate a complex court process. as well as making sure the voices of children could be heard above the noise of adults.

I had amazing support throughout this period from government ministers, civil servants, my own board, my own workforce and – above all – judges. Whenever I was in a trench, I took a judge with me, as they knew better than anyone else how to get out. The leading family judges in the country only got together once a year. Quite a few times, I had to run the gauntlet and persuade them to back me.

I learnt that change is impossible unless the major players in any system agree the operating environment together. Anyone can agree and sign off strategy, but changing a system and culture is much more complex.

The devil is always in the detail, so I learnt to go straight to the detail, as well as to change the operating model in Cafcass and give judges what they wanted – concise, evidence-based reports with clear recommendations and an early opinion about what is best for the child rather than lacking in professional confidence and trying to keep everyone happy by sitting on the fence until the end, thereby allowing less time for negotiation and dialogue between all of the parties in a case.

Relative stability (2012–2019)

I can recall the earlier tipping point into chaos vividly, but I cannot recall the tipping point of improvement – when we began to produce good work most of the time. I do remember the feeling more than the facts.

Gradually, life became easier and often enjoyable rather than messy and permanently anxious. In this period, I learnt the importance of happiness in work. We became proud of what we were doing. We were getting better feedback – not from everyone, but enough to prove we were on the right track.

I was on a lecture tour in New Zealand in 2014 when my operational director – an amazing manager who has inspired so many others in her career – rang me in the middle of the New Zealand night to say our leadership judgement in a national Ofsted inspection had been moderated up from good to outstanding. I did not like the crude grading system until I came out on top, and then I loved it. This gave us all a boost, and we drove ourselves to achieve an all-round outstanding grade in our next full inspection in 2018.

At that point, I decided to leave. I felt I had taken Cafcass from being one of the worst organizations in the public sector to one of the best. It was time to see if I could do anything else.

Reflections for relational leadership

As the service leader, I had to be aware of the image I was projecting and how I was being perceived by my staff, the board and our many stakeholders. This went beyond managing my reputation and instead was about staying in active contact with the whole organization both face to face and virtually to know how I was impacting cultural change.

I visited each of our local offices at least twice a year, which meant I was usually travelling around the country for three days a week. At the same time, I had to keep in touch with a constantly changing number of individuals who were important at a single point in time, who came and went from my world. If one of my relationships fractured, I had to repair it.

My staff told me that they felt heard, listened to and motivated by me and that I created a connection with them. Remembering names and personal details was important, as it showed that everyone mattered. On many days, I spent my time from the start to finish of the working day speaking with my own staff and with stakeholders, which was quite a feat, as I avoid small talk outside work.

Relational leadership was the oil lubricating our performance engine.

I often say that if I had my time again, I would be able to turn Cafcass around in half the time, even though fundamental improvement takes years, not months. But is this true?

I would try to solve the underlying problems I was firefighting much earlier, but then, I was spending every day firefighting, which left no time for dealing with the underlying issues.

I would be ruthless about what needed to be changed earlier and not so worried about short-term consequences, but leadership is a fragile business, where a leader can often not recover from a huge error of judgement made in haste.

If I had my time again, I like to think I would achieve more day by day rather than starting each working day with a to-do list that grew longer by the end of the day as if I had done nothing for ten hours. In fact, I was always doing 'stuff', non-stop, just to keep the show on the road.

So, it is impossible to say I could have done better, but it is enough for me to know that we helped many thousands of children during my time.

I now work internationally. The issues for children and families are much the same across the world even if the politics are poles apart. No country has managed to get children's services right. It is unrealistic to believe that any service can venture into the darkest areas of human existence without causing collateral damage. I have to constantly remind myself that supporting babies, children, young people and their families does often make the difference between an individual or a family's collapse or survival.

That for me is the main lesson, and the simplest one of all – that children are usually helped most by helping their families and that, in turn, those who help them are saints, not sinners.

REFLECTIONS

I now pose three questions about relational leadership, in the spirit of learning and reflection.

1. As a leader, how can you establish instant rapport with your staff?
2. How can you persuade and influence the staff you manage to follow you and your vision?
3. How can you build a high-trust, high-performance culture from scratch?

• Chapter 2 •

LEADERSHIP AND VULNERABILITY

Peter Buzzi and Claudia Megele

Dr Peter Buzzi is a leading authority in safeguarding, wellbeing and restorative trauma-informed approaches. He is the Director of the Centre for Safeguarding and Wellbeing Practice and Research and the Chair of the Interdisciplinary Association of Safeguarding Professionals. With a career spanning national and international contexts, Peter has led major research and transformation programmes across the public and private sectors in the UK, US, Japan and Europe. His work includes inter-governmental knowledge transfer initiatives and he is currently leading a research and practice development project in England, in partnership with several local authorities. Peter's work focuses on creating meaningful change through relational, evidence-informed approaches that support systems transformation and organizational development and wellbeing.

Claudia Megele is the Director of Quality, Safety, Improvement and Safeguarding in the States of Guernsey (the Channel Islands). She has held several leadership roles in different local authorities and national organizations in the UK including Assistant Director and National Safeguarding Lead for Cafcass and the National Chair of the Principal Social Workers Network. She has also led multiple research projects and is Fellow of the National Institute for Health Research (NIHR). Claudia has also advised and led various boards including as the Chair of Tower Hamlets Police and Community Safety Board, member of the advisory board of the National Children's Bureau (NCB) and Trustee at Mind.

In this chapter, we use the pronoun 'I' when an experience or event relates to one of the authors only.

Introduction

So much has been said about vulnerability and the importance of embracing our vulnerability and yet, at least in the workplace, most people feel uncomfortable about sharing or demonstrating their vulnerability.

In this chapter, we argue that our difficulty in acknowledging and showing our vulnerability in general, and vulnerability in the workplace in particular, lies in a misunderstanding of vulnerability, and we offer an alternative approach to vulnerability that views it as a gateway to growth and integral to power.

Vulnerability and emotionally exposed leadership

For decades, we have collectively been dependent on outdated leadership stereotypes and on the notion that vulnerability is weakness. In fact, in its issue of 4 October 1993, *Fortune* magazine (Deseret News, 1993) crowned the 'roughest, toughest, most intimidating bosses', stating that T. J. Rodgers, head of Cypress Semiconductor, put on what he called a 'drooling psycho face' to harangue employees and that Warnaco's chief executive officer, Linda Wachner, once kept an executive waiting for three days and then dismissed him after a two-minute meeting.

She was also reported as telling an executive, 'You'd better start firing people so they'll understand you're serious', while Steve Jobs was said to have addressed workers in a way that some newspapers could only describe as '!$&?+!%/;)!' (*ibid.*).

These examples reflect a harsh and oppressive culture of 'command and control' that was perpetuated by fear and sustained by a crushing imbalance of power and rigid hierarchies. This fear-driven culture is exemplified by the quote above: 'You'd better start firing people so they'll understand you're serious.' Clearly, in such a predatory and fear-based culture, there could be no room for any expression, much less acknowledgement, of any vulnerability.

Fast forward to today's workplace where organizations are more laterally structured with reduced hierarchies. Boundaries begin to become looser and break down between different departments and different job categories (manager, professional, technical, etc.) as different parts of the organization need to share knowledge and co-work together to achieve shared objectives. This blurring of boundaries also affects organizational roles.

As employees gain greater flexibility, autonomy and decisional authority, managers become more of a coach or facilitator and social supporter rather than a commander. In this environment, workers are no longer managed to comply with rules and orders but rather to be committed to the organizational goals and mission.

A culture of fear at best leads to compulsion, not motivation, and hierarchies at best lead to compliance, not connection. But in today's workplace, people are driven by choice and motivation rather than fear and compulsion and seek connection and belonging rather than hierarchy and control. Indeed, their emotions and the way people feel about their work have a significant impact on their productivity and performance and, hence, a direct impact on organizational success and the success of organizational leadership. This highlights the importance of emotional leadership and the inevitability of emotional exposure in leadership.

Unfortunately, however, the influence and practices of outdated fear-based leadership styles and command-and-control culture are still observable in many public sector organizations. This is compounded by the structures, dynamics and constraints that influence and differentiate the workplace environment from other non-work-related experiences. So, how does workplace vulnerability differ from the non-work environment?

To be vulnerable

Most people have experienced vulnerability and know what it feels like to feel vulnerable.

Most people may have shown or shared their vulnerability at home with their children, family or friends as a way of connecting and bonding or generating better understanding, or to show or solicit sympathy or empathy. Most of us recognize the power and importance of vulnerability and the sharing of vulnerability to build and maintain trust and relationships. In fact, we don't feel a strong sense of connection with people who don't show any vulnerability and don't share anything about themselves. To build trust, we need to make ourselves vulnerable by giving something of ourselves.

Although we may appreciate the power and significance of vulnerability, we might not be comfortable sharing or showing our vulnerability at the workplace. After all, there are different dynamics and expectations at the workplace. There are hierarchies and power differences; there are employees, deadlines, clients with different requirements, multiple job demands, different organizational structures, varying expectations, rewards and repercussions that condition our behaviours, relationships and identities and everything that happens at the workplace.

Holding a formal leadership position can further complicate the situation, as we are responsible for others and for what happens in our team and their collective performance. We hold a wide range of responsibilities, from employees' performance and motivation to budget and fiscal aspects of the team and important 'soft issues' such as health and wellbeing. So not only is vulnerability in the workplace not the same as vulnerability in a non-work environment, but being a formal leader in the workplace also adds further constraints and expectations that are not the same for everyone else.

This raises two important questions.

First, is vulnerability inevitable for leaders in general and in the workplace in particular?

And if the answer is yes, how can we show vulnerability in a way that enhances our impact, influence and leadership rather than undermining it?

Is vulnerability inevitable?

Whether we operate as an individual practitioner or lead a large organization, we all face challenges and uncertainties and operate in a complex and often fast-changing and volatile environment. Therefore, we are all vulnerable to changing circumstances, challenges we don't anticipate, outcomes we don't expect and multiple demands, pressures and expectations. Therefore, whether we recognize it and are willing to acknowledge it or not, vulnerability is a fact of life, and we are all vulnerable in multiple ways.

Therefore, the question is not whether or not we are vulnerable. The true question is whether or not we care enough and have the courage to acknowledge and recognize our own vulnerability and that of others.

This is a question about self-awareness. Do we want to go through life blindfolded in order to suppress who we are and not see our vulnerabilities? Or do we care enough to face ourselves and to acknowledge and recognize our vulnerabilities so we can prepare and better navigate the challenges, uncertainties and complexities of life and today's workplace?

The currency of vulnerability

So, does accepting and sharing or showing our vulnerability help us become better leaders, strengthen our bonds and motivate others?

To answer that question, imagine being on a ship in the middle of a stormy ocean with waves breaking over the deck and the ship rocking violently. You look at the captain and trust his abilities, hoping that he knows what he is doing. Now, imagine that the captain makes an announcement: 'I know you are anxious and worried, and to tell the truth, I am quite anxious and worried myself. So I understand your feelings and hope that acknowledging our vulnerability makes you feel better.'

The captain has acknowledged his vulnerability, but instead of creating greater connection, trust and comfort, his words might result in panic among the passengers. So what is missing?

Vulnerability is one side of the coin. The other side of the coin is what it can offer, which is the possibility of learning, growth and development. Figure 2.1, 'The Double Helix of Exposure and Expansion', demonstrates the two sides of the coin. The captain projected the exposure, or vulnerability, side of the coin without expansion, or the growth side of the coin.

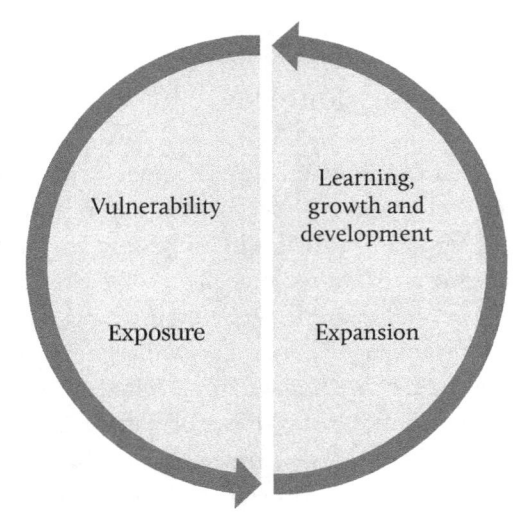

FIGURE 2.1: THE DOUBLE HELIX OF EXPOSURE AND EXPANSION
Source: Peter Buzzi and Claudia Megele

If we wish to *use* the currency of vulnerability effectively, we need to present the full coin and ensure that exposure is accompanied by expansion. In other words, speaking of vulnerability and exposure alone is fine in a therapeutic setting, but even then the journey of healing begins when we recognize its potential for expansion and begin to realize the growth side of vulnerability. When we express vulnerability to create connection, and especially purposeful connections, we need to show the growth and development side of the coin as well. For example, the captain could have said, 'I know you are anxious and worried. This is a natural reaction to this kind of storm, and to tell the truth, I also feel anxious at times, but I channel my anxiety to create greater focus and to get through the storm. I know this looks bad, but we have been through many such storms and have navigated safely out of it. So let's keep calm and focused.'

Here the captain acknowledges the challenge ahead and shares his own vulnerability and experience of fear, but he accompanies that with a reassuring vision that fosters confidence and demonstrates leadership.

To use the currency of vulnerability, we need to acknowledge the challenges and the difficult circumstances while offering a vision and a way forward that leads to learning, growth, development and strength. Figure 2.2, 'The Growth Loop', highlights the steps involved in tapping into the power of vulnerability and achieving its potential. We can think of this approach as a five-step process:

1. **Face the truth:** The first step is to acknowledge the vulnerability.

2. **Spot the spark:** The second step is to recognize and identify its potential for learning, growth and development.

3. **Chart the course:** The third step is to plan and outline in measurable terms how to realize that potential.

4. **Walk the walk:** The fourth step is to act on what we have planned. This can be daunting at times, as change doesn't come easy, and it is often easier to fall back on old habits. So acting on our plan with commitment, constancy and consistency is key to harnessing the promise and potential of vulnerability.

5. **Check and charge up:** The fifth step is to evaluate and monitor our progress and to celebrate our achievements as we move along the path of realizing the potential of our vulnerability while remembering that no achievement is too small to celebrate.

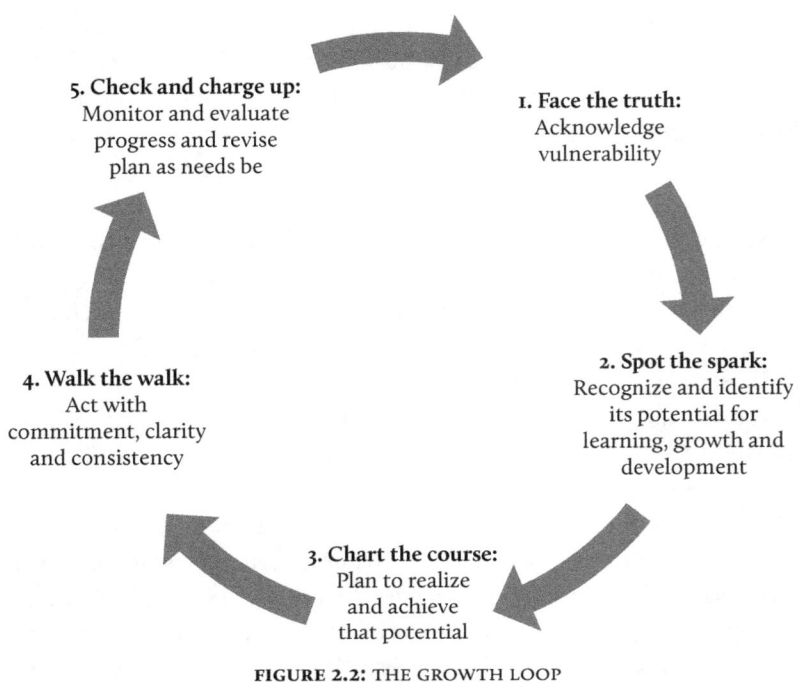

5. Check and charge up: Monitor and evaluate progress and revise plan as needs be

1. Face the truth: Acknowledge vulnerability

2. Spot the spark: Recognize and identify its potential for learning, growth and development

3. Chart the course: Plan to realize and achieve that potential

4. Walk the walk: Act with commitment, clarity and consistency

FIGURE 2.2: THE GROWTH LOOP
Source: Peter Buzzi and Claudia Megele

When we face vulnerability, especially in the workplace, we can take a step back to reflect on its potential for learning, growth and development. Even when faced with a significant setback or failure, we can indicate what we've learnt from that experience and what we can do to mitigate or prevent similar occurrences in the future. Indeed, when thinking about our own growth and development, it can be said that most often we have learnt more from our setbacks, failures and other difficult experiences than most other experiences in our lives.

> **Case example**: Excellence without vulnerability is a label devoid of meaning
> In a leadership training session with a local authority's children's services rated as outstanding by Ofsted, one of the senior managers stated, 'I have an open-door policy, and anyone can come to me to raise issues. I encourage people to talk about their difficulties and to come to me but they don't. What do you do in that sort of situation?'
> My response to that question was: 'Make yourself human. Make sure the people see the person behind the title.'

Often, in the workplace, when people encounter a person from higher levels of the organizational hierarchy and when there is a significant power differential between people, what they see is the person's title rather than the person.

Imagine the director or CEO of an organization visiting a frontline team. The talk within the team could be: 'Oh, be careful, the director is coming to our team today.' Such a statement suggests a lack of connection with the director – that what people see is 'the director' and the power associated with that title and not the person. This, at best, can lead to compliance but doesn't engender connection. To connect and lead from connection, people need to see the *human* behind the title. This is what I mean by 'Make yourself human'.

However, if we want others to see the human behind the title, we need to communicate it – by behaving humanely and demonstrating and acknowledging humanity and vulnerability.

In subsequent discussions in that training session, it became evident that the focus on narratives of strength and excellence didn't leave any room for reflection or expression of vulnerability. It also became evident that the organization was struggling with retention of staff and that the quality of practice had begun to deteriorate.

This highlights that without making ourselves vulnerable and allowing for reflection, even what is perceived as a point of organizational strength can become a distraction and hindrance to effective leadership and growth.

In this case, the organizational leadership's focus on strength and excellence had left no room for reflection and expression of vulnerabilities – the difficulties and challenges that inevitably arise and exist in every organization. The organizational leadership had become self-obsessed with the label of 'outstanding' to the extent that it had lost its focus on the elements that would lead to becoming 'outstanding'. In suppressing their own fears and vulnerabilities, the organizational leaders projected a narrative of strength without an acknowledgement of the challenges, concerns and vulnerabilities that do inevitably arise and exist in every organization and relationship.

As a result, managers and staff felt like the act of raising or discussing any issues or concerns would be perceived as weakness and would negatively impact others' assessment of their image, identity and performance.

It also led to a loss of connection between staff and the organization, creating a high-pressure environment that alienated both managers and staff. This loss of connection in turn resulted in a loss of valuable staff and hampered organizational learning and development.

Without the humility to acknowledge and accept our vulnerability, there is no possibility for connection or reflection and no room for learning or improvement, let alone excellence.

Case example: Leading through vulnerability for a new strategy

The Covid-19 pandemic resulted in widespread uncertainties and feelings of vulnerability across services. During this time, I was the assistant director in a national organization with responsibility for hundreds of staff and a wide geographic area of operation encompassing some of the largest local authorities in the country, in addition to being the national safeguarding lead for the organization.

We were experiencing intense and increasing demand on services, with nearly double the demand in some areas, and the situation and the workload for my team was clearly unsustainable. I was working in a large and complex system with statutory responsibilities and a highly structured and hierarchical setting. We needed urgent change in strategy and operation, but change can be painstakingly slow in such a large and complex organization.

This was a moment of great personal, professional and organizational vulnerability, and often our response to vulnerability is one of denial or a narrow focus on action. Therefore, I needed to arrive at a shared understanding with all stakeholders, including service users, the CEO, the director, my peers, managers, practitioners, local authorities, the judiciary and others. The shared recognition of the vulnerabilities of the existing system served as a point of departure and, through numerous meetings and consultations, we were able to identify and agree on essential elements that could ensure we would meet our statutory responsibilities and the safety and safeguarding needs of people who accessed our services.

As Peter Drucker suggests, 'The first step in a growth policy is not to decide where and how to grow. It is to decide what to abandon' (Parmenter, 2012, p.74).

This was a moment of great vulnerability, and by acknowledging those vulnerabilities and through collaboration and reflection, we were able to create a new prioritization strategy and operational growth and sustainability policy, which was subsequently adapted and applied across the organization.

The myth of power and vulnerability

Vulnerability is about that part of ourselves that can expose us to added emotional labour or increased risk of harm or undesirable outcomes. Being vulnerable is about sharing the authentic part of ourselves that we may have otherwise chosen to hide or keep private. Therefore, showing vulnerability is a personal choice, rather than a skill, that requires the self-awareness to ask: Will being open and honest in this moment serve me? Will it serve others?

From a psychoanalytic perspective, our vulnerabilities and unconscious fear of death can present such powerful and unbearable challenge that we project such fears and vulnerabilities onto others and, in doing so, construct and idolize an imagined omnipotence.

In this yearning for omnipotence, we create heroes and superheroes who epitomize power and invincibility. And yet, each of these imagined heroes, from Ulysses and Hercules to Superman and other superheroes, has some point of vulnerability.

Even Achilles, the Greek mythological archetype of power and invincibility, had his heel that led to his downfall. The legend goes that Achilles gained near invincibility because his mother, Thetis, dipped him in the River Styx, but his heel, where his mother held him, was covered by her hand and so remained untouched by the river and became his point of vulnerability.

Have you ever wondered why? Why not create a hero or superhero that is all-powerful and invincible without any vulnerability?

The answer may be that although we idolize their power, it is their vulnerability that makes them relatable. We relate and connect with our heroes through their vulnerability, and without it, we wouldn't feel the same sense of connection. Indeed, the myth of power, invulnerability and invincibility has carried with it its own contradiction right from the start, as vulnerability is not the opposite of power – it is the gateway to power, and integral to it. However, to tap into the power of vulnerability, we need to recognize and realize its promise and potential as a gateway for learning, growth, development and strength.

REFLECTIONS

1. What do you consider to be your three greatest vulnerabilities and what do others see as your three greatest vulnerabilities? Are there any differences between your view and the views of others? If yes, what does this difference represent and what are its implications?
2. How do your own vulnerabilities influence your thinking, feelings, relationships, actions and decisions?
3. How can you acknowledge and demonstrate/share your own and others' vulnerabilities within professional boundaries in order to enable learning, growth and development? Consider how vulnerability can foster a sense of belonging and strengthen your relational leadership bonds.

References

Deseret News (1993) Magazine Crowns 7 'Roughest, Toughest Bosses'. www.deseret.com/1993/9/30/19068505/magazine-crowns-7-roughest-toughest-bosses

Parmenter, D. (2012) *Key Performance Indicators for Government and Non Profit Agencies: Implementing Winning KPIs.* Hoboken, NJ: John Wiley and Sons.

• Chapter 3 •

LEADING COMPLEXITY

Tanya Moore

> Dr Tanya Moore is a social work practitioner, leader and academic. She's currently Principal Social Worker for Essex Adult Care Services and Doctoral Supervisor at the Tavistock and Portman NHS Foundation Trust.

Introduction

Senior leaders can lead change but we can't control it. This chapter tells the story of my own experience of a change process in the introduction of a new practice model to a local authority adult care service.

I consider how plans introduced by senior leaders can be stalled by unpredictable events and by the unseen relational dynamics that are part of every organization. And I show how complexity theory helped me understand how organizations both resist and protect themselves from change. Ultimately though, I suggest that change must be supported by relationally informed leadership that demonstrates understanding and respect for the people who make up an organization and for the feelings they bring with them.

Complexity theory challenges the Newtonian principle of 'cause and effect', offering a different set of rules to understand how complex organisms, such as social care departments, work. It recognizes the existence of 'complex adaptive systems', which are networks of dynamic agents whose interactions can create unpredictable change. Examples include the climate, animal swarms, power grids, the ocean and groups of people such as businesses, schools and even families.

'Emergence' is where parts of the system react to each other and create a status that wouldn't be created by individual behaviours. It's a pattern of actions that develop over time in response to unexpected opportunities and challenges. Unlike linear strategies, which are a predefined series of sequential steps leading to an ultimate goal, emergent strategies form organically from within a system as it adapts to the changes in its environment.

A high-profile example of this is the Tesco Clubcard, which was originally introduced as a simple loyalty card, but its response to changing expectation and opportunity means it now tracks individual shopping habits and makes personalized offers. The new emergence is its potential for use in public health, as it can notice when shoppers' baskets are becoming unhealthy and 'nudge' them through personalized offers into making healthier choices.

Emergence is a significant phenomenon with creative potential, but to benefit, the whole system must be seen, because focusing on the trees comes at the cost of seeing the wood. It was Tesco's view of wider system themes leading to emerging opportunity that highlighted its loyalty card's potential for both commercial personalization and public health.

With or without a change programme, change is constant. Its drivers are the relationships between internal, external and inter-facing elements. Despite the attempts of linear 'command and control' approaches to leadership and service planning, the future can never be accurately predicted, and history can never be reversed.

Complicated systems such as engines might be large or intricate but they're built to a design, so with sufficient technical knowledge they can be predicted and understood. Complexity doesn't seek an overall planned design; it recognizes constant, unpredictable change.

Complexity challenges traditional assumptions that observed effects have observable causes, that analysis of past events will help predict future events and that complicated phenomena can be understood by breaking the whole into parts and analysing them (The Health Foundation, 2010). On the contrary, analysis of the parts would be considered to be at the cost of a view of the connections between them.

Complexity looks instead at the relationships and interactions *within and between* organizations (Vada, 2015).

Xshire: a complex adaptive system

Xshire is the local authority where I spent four years as head of social work and then principal social worker.

It's no coincidence that I view the local authority in terms of relationships. I've worked in or alongside this organization for much of my career, and in a previous role as lecturer on a social work qualifying course, I taught many of its social workers. So my view of the organization is essentially relational.

In complexity terms, Xshire is a 'complex adaptive system'. It's open to a continual flow of members including workers, clients, managers, directors, partner organizations, politicians, subcontractors and others. There are always people joining and leaving the system. Evolving membership alone means constant change, but Xshire is also subject to strong external pressures such as financial, political and policy steers and, of course, significant events like the external and internally driven impact of the Covid-19 pandemic.

This non-stop ebb of new people, ideas and influences creates a 'stasis of emergence' – a situation in which emergence is constant, where new patterns, trends or emotions are constantly materializing.

Planning in Xshire must account for its scale and geography. Its adult care department covers 40+ social work teams as well as numerous business and support services that need to be held within any communication across its significant geographical reach. Each of these teams has its own microculture with both internal and external influences. The relationships between each of these teams' members internally and each of the teams externally influence the collective behaviours of the system and the emergence of new aspects of the system.

The new practice model

The call from the Care Act (Department of Health and Social Care, 2014) for a shift from 'care management', in which the social care practitioner is positioned as the 'expert' who assesses and determines the needs of the person, to relationship and strengths-based practice, in which the person and practitioner work in partnership to consider what might be most helpful, was a major driver for change.

Xshire's response was to introduce a three-stage model consisting of:

1. short encounter/conversation between the person and practitioner leading to immediate information or assistance
2. short-term but more substantial contact to help the person regain control of their situation
3. ongoing support.

The underpinning philosophy is that people's own relationships, connections and ideas for their lives are likely to be more sustainable than any a service might introduce, so unnecessary dependence and risk aversion should be avoided. In complexity terms, provision of care and support from an outside agency might seem to address a problem but might introduce another agent adding new complexities to the system.

For example, arranging home care to help a person manage their morning shower might solve an immediate difficulty but this might also cause issues for other family members who have to tolerate a stranger in their home at a busy time of day. It might cause a new dependency in the person who was sort of managing before, and this might cause a problem when there's no carer available. Alternatively, support from an occupational therapist might help the person find an easier way (perhaps with equipment) to manage their shower themselves.

As leaders, it's tempting to believe that a well-planned and executed strategy based upon a Newtonian understanding of cause and predictable effect would do the trick. For example, in the introduction of a new practice model in an adult social care setting, a period of consultation might be followed by the launching of practice principles, training programmes and introduction of the new recording requirements. This might be cascaded from senior managers to team managers through to the teams.

But it's never that simple. Systems have history and memory, and these can impact any attempts to create change.

Xshire had benefited from a previous practice campaign within its disability services. A series of compelling speakers had been brought in for lunchtime lectures. Practitioners had been introduced to strengths-based approaches and encouraged to work with local communities to explore sources of natural support that might be a more natural fit for a person needing help than social care. In complexity terms, these actions were 'catalytic probes' or 'safe to fail' experiments (Snowden, 2016); this attempt to create change might have caused a significant improvement in the service, but even if it failed, it would have created learning rather than harm.

Complexity theory would suggest innovation can't be created; we can only create the conditions that allow it to emerge. In this case, practitioners were invited to think outside the confines of their previous care management role, and this created an emergence of practitioner champions who led on a shift in practice focus from within the teams. Their creative response to the catalytic probes saw the emergence of community and citizen-based projects such as a disability arts festival and a support group for transgender people and their families.

But complex systems can't be predicted, and what worked in one situation won't necessarily work in another. A similar project launched for older people's services wasn't so warmly received. This might have been because of the different nature of the work, the differing expectations of the people being supported or a different relationship with the leading officer. Each part of a complex adaptive system responds differently (*ibid.*) and the form of this response can't always be predicted.

The 'holy grail' of standardized practice across a service will always remain elusive. A hospital social work team that's part of the wider adult care service may be working to the visible pressure of patients on stretchers in the corridor whilst waiting for beds to become available. They will have a different view of the organization to the community-based social workers engaging in long-term individual work and stimulating community capacity. We might implement a standardized governance structure but locally valid solutions will always emerge, and complexity tells us our challenge is to learn from and work with these differences.

Complex systems are resistant to efforts to change them, and organizations have strong conscious or unconscious will to maintain an equilibrium. Despite this, the 'stasis of nostalgic fantasy' (Moore, 2021), where we imagine there was once a time of no change, can only ever have been a fantasy, as organizations continue to evolve, so an established member of staff going on maternity leave will come back to an altered team, and the change can never be reversed.

Complexity theory suggests we need an emergent strategy to *work with* the flow of change rather than an attempt to impose pre-designed ideas on complex organizations. The new Xshire practice model introduced blank forms instead of tick boxes for recording its assessments. This meant assessment conversations could be directed by what's most important to the person instead of what's asked by the form. Management sign-off was removed from the assessment, as well as for any expenditure of up to £500.

Our intention was to liberate practitioners from unnecessary forms and enable them to make independent decisions. But in the high-anxiety world of social care, a reliance upon tick boxes is about more than a gathering of information; it represents a belief that predefined procedures will avert risk. There's some truth in this for closed systems. For example, the procedure of counting in and counting out surgical instruments in an operating theatre is widely understood to save lives. But instrument checklists alone can't prevent mishaps: disrespect for junior staff, inadequate training and frequent staff changes (all indicators of a complex system) are also seen to contribute to lack of theatre safety (NHS England, 2014).

For the open systems that are people's lives, simple actions can't guarantee risk reduction, and protection from risk can be a risk in itself (Duffy and Sutton, 2018, p.54).

Alongside the launch of the practice model, we staged a recruitment drive that began with a Saturday open day offering on-the-spot interviews. Our eye-catching posters and social media posts promised to 'deal with the paperwork later' and offered a day of continuing professional development sessions, interview coaching and cake.

This was another catalytic probe – an initiative that would not have a significant negative impact if it were to fail. Our thinking was that even if no one came to the open day, there would have been good publicity created in the build-up. But the day was an unanticipated success, and 32 job offers were made.

We've since considered what went so right. Complexity tells us it was a happy example of emergence: the timing, the social media, the new practice model may have all played their part but so might the good weather and the announcement of additional financial pressures in a neighbouring authority.

It isn't possible to identify the exact ingredients of success, and although we've tried to repeat the formula, complexity would dismiss a linear suggestion that full understanding can be gained by analytical reductionism. So it wasn't just the identifiable elements of the recruitment event but the relationship between those and other unidentified elements that created such beneficial emergence.

Disappointingly, we've never repeated our 32 appointments high, so whether it was the newness, the timing or the 'likes' gained on social media, the emergence experienced here was based on more than coaching and cake.

Defences

Social work organizations have been criticized for being procedurally focused (Munro, 2010) and for introducing new procedures each time something goes wrong.

The result is a defensive system that assumes strict adherence to procedure will avert risk. But there's always scope for the unpredicted to happen in social care organizations. While social workers are investing their time in gathering information to demonstrate consideration of all risk, they will have less time available to *do social work* – to engage with people in a meaningful way to understand what's important to them. It's impossible to avert all risk, and most of us would recognize the presence of reasonable risk in a well-lived life and in professional practice.

In anticipating the risks attached to the launch of the new model, the removal of management sign-off for Care Act assessments and the devolved spending authority caused the most anxiety – would the budget be blown?

In fact, although most managers did relinquish ownership of their team's assessments, there were reports that some still insisted on reviewing them before they could be finalized. This expression of managerial anxiety may have had sound reasons; where a team is short-staffed or relying on new or temporary staff, it would be a reasonable response for the manager to want to assert more vigilance.

Our attempt to 'command and control' on this new approach to management sign-off hadn't worked, and despite the complete redesign of the underpinning IT system, those teams that weren't able to cope with the intended change were finding local ways to thwart it.

Complexity tells us that attempts to break down silos in a complex adaptive system are likely to fail and a more realistic approach is to recognize their existence and work with them to set a direction of travel rather than a goal (Snowden, 2016).

Instead of laying out practice ultimatums to the reluctant managers, we worked with the flow of change, marking out a clear direction of travel but allowing other change drivers such as the expectations of new team members to create change over time.

Complexity recognizes that organizations have internal processes that enable them to survive change. Social services departments in the UK have been subjected to repeated budget cuts, reorganizations and changes in ideological drive yet are, arguably, still broadly recognizable. This 'autopoiesis', or ability of an organization to maintain its existing form despite changes in conditions, is seen by complexity to be a resilience as well as an obstruction. 'Slash and burn' approaches to change risk losing what's good about a service. Teams that hold together are to be respected and nurtured.

The need for psychoanalytical understanding

Autonomy requires trust, confidence and an ability to tolerate a level of anxiety. For some teams, the removal of management endorsement from assessments was a sticking point.

The guiding rationale was that social workers 'own' their assessments and make reasonable decisions about allocating resources so managers don't double up on this work. The anticipation was that cutting out the management would result in speedier responses for clients and save time for workers and managers, freeing them for more creative endeavours.

But, as discussed, for some, relinquishing this responsibility caused anxiety. It's a common mistake to ignore how human resistances and responses will impact organizational change (Bovey and Hede, 2001) and complexity doesn't do this; its strength is partially its recognition and approach to working with the unpredictable but also its recognition of the impact of emotions and relationships on organizations.

For me, there's helpful understanding in Menzies' (1960) description of unconscious anxieties amongst hospital nursing staff and the defence mechanisms employed to protect the staff from the painful realities of their work. Menzies' study of a hospital nursing service concluded that working in health and social care organizations causes significant anxiety. She noted the function of, for example, ritual task performance and checks and counterchecks of decisions as a defence against the difficult emotion of the task. Just as the nurses in Menzies' study sought refuge from the emotion of their work in the depersonalization of nursing tasks, so the busy social work managers struggle to let go of the unnecessary administrative aspects of their role.

The same anxiety is experienced by some social workers in the removal of tick-box assessment forms. The maligned bureaucratic processes of care management served an unconscious function of defending practitioners and managers against their own anxious responses to the difficult work of social care. Stripped of its tick boxes and questionnaires, the new practice model recording system exposes practitioners to authentic relationship-based practice and the costly personal investment this demands from both client and worker and also demands of the organization if it's to support its staff to offer such a rich but demanding approach to practice.

The introduction of the new model in Xshire was largely successful. The Adult Social Care Outcomes Framework results showed a pleasing year-on-year improvement, and the annual Employer Standards Health Check presented a focused, purposeful and largely stable professional workforce.

Our experience in Xshire found complexity's acknowledgement of continual evolution to be a helpful framework for strategic thinking and planning but it stopped short of understanding the causes of resistance and the impact of anxiety that change necessarily provokes. Relationally informed leadership fills this gap, offering authentic understanding and respect of the organization and its emotional dynamics.

Effective leaders in the public sector don't buy into the simple fantasy of top-down control. They work with the reality of the unseen and the unexpected, acknowledging and appreciating the emotions and relationships that make up an organization. Such combination of theoretical and relational understanding can offer a clear view of complexity.

REFLECTIONS

1. What are the main drivers within the complex adaptive system that is your organization?
2. In what ways has your organization benefited from unforeseen creative emergence?
3. What are likely to be the main causes for resistance for programmes of change within your organization?

References

Bovey, W. H. and Hede, A. (2001) 'Resistance to organisational change: The role of defence mechanisms.' *Journal of Managerial Psychology 16,* 7, 534–548.
Department of Health and Social Care (2014) *The Care Act.* London: Her Majesty's Stationery Office. Retrieved from *Care Act 2014* (legislation.gov.uk).
Duffy, S. and Sutton, J. (2018) 'Working with Risk.' In D. Ford (ed.) *Working with Complexity: Evidence Review.* Research in Practice for Adults.
Menzies, I. E. P. (1960) 'A case-study in the functioning of social systems as a defence against anxiety: A report on a study of the nursing service of a general hospital.' *Human Relations 13,* 2, 95–121.

Moore, T. (2021) 'Complex and conscious. Case study of a change programme in a UK local authority adult care service through a complexity and psychoanalytical lens.' *Journal of Social Work Practice 35*, 1, 39–50.

Munro, E. (2010) *The Munro Review of Child Protection – Part One: A Systems Analysis*. London: Department for Education.

NHS England (2014) *Standardise, educate, harmonise. Commissioning the conditions for safer surgery Summary of the report of the NHS England Never Events Taskforce.* https://www.england.nhs.uk/wp-content/uploads/2014/02/sur-nev-ev-tf-rep.pdf

Snowden, D. J. (2016, July 21–26) *How leaders change culture through small actions.* [Presentation]. AcademiWales Summer School 2016, Cardiff. https://www.youtube.com/watch?v=MsLmjoAp_Dg

The Health Foundation (2010) *Complex adaptive systems.* https://www.health.org.uk/reports-and-analysis/reports/complex-adaptive-systems

Vada, Ø. (2015) 'Leadership in a Complex World – A Conceptual Framework.' In: F. Heylighen, C. Joslyn and V. Turchin (eds) *Principia Cybernetica Web* (Principia Cybernetica, Brussels). http://pespmc1.vub.ac.be/ECCO/Oyvind/Oyvind-LeadershipComplexWorld.pdf

• Chapter 4 •

USING COMMUNICATION TO LEAD CHANGE

Anna Korving

> Anna Korving is an e-entrepreneur and senior business communications leader who mentors senior leaders and has led businesses and teams across the public relations, medical communications and healthcare advertising space in London and New York.

Change is personal

Change is always personal. For the people leading the change, for the people who have to deal with the consequences of change and for those we ask to implement that change on our behalf.

As leaders, the way in which we communicate around change is crucial to its success at every level. In this chapter, I outline some practical steps to consider when leading change communications but also some of the ways in which leaders can enable those around us to embrace it.

As a sibling carer, I'd like to begin with an example that's very close to home. Five years ago, then in his late 50s, my brother moved into a supported living facility after being looked after by my parents for the whole of his life. It was a massive upheaval, and the transition was not without its challenges, but with the help of a great team of support workers, his life has been transformed. He is empowered to do the things he wants to do, feels successful and has so much more independence and choice about his future. As a family, we had spent a long time searching for the right place for my brother, finally settling upon one of the Camphill Village Trust communities, which support people with learning disabilities, autism and mental health challenges to lead a life of opportunity.

It was a search we had embarked upon with great apprehension, because everything we knew about supported living was based on an outdated understanding of care models. To find somewhere that actively encouraged people to make their own choices, had a robust approach to safeguarding and took a long-term view of the needs and potential of the individuals they support was somewhat of a surprise. Clearly, models of care had changed significantly over the many years since the question of my brother's long-term future had first been raised. So had the organizations that delivered support.

The Camphill Village Trust itself has grown and evolved over the 75+ years since its foundation and now runs nine communities across the UK as well as offering significant day services for non-residents. It is constantly adapting to meet the needs of its communities, supporting the co-development of services with the people it supports. As a family member, I was invited last year to attend a meeting with their CEO, Sara Thakkar. She had taken up the role some months previously in the midst of the pandemic, and this was a first opportunity for us to meet her and understand her vision for the future of the organization. Some family members had been involved with the community for decades and had lived through much change in recent years, so for them, a lot was riding on this first encounter.

It was a masterclass in change communication as well as in relational leadership. The new CEO was calm and composed, her body language was open and she had the answers to all the questions raised at her fingertips. She had obviously worked closely with her senior leadership team in preparing for the meeting and brought them into the discussion as equals. She listened carefully, tuning in to the emotion of her audience before giving thoughtful responses, and was comfortable in saying no as well as yes to some enquiries. This acted to enhance her credibility and gravitas, as she wasn't just telling people what they wanted to hear but had a clear vision and direction for the future that she was laying out in front of them. As a result, I and others came away reassured that the person leading the organization was highly skilled, highly professional and 'all over' their brief – even if some didn't agree with everything she had to say.

This was a great example of a leader who had taken time to consider, understand and prepare for an interaction that would set the tone for the future. This moment of communication was a fulcrum – sealing the commitment of her team to what had been agreed whilst at the same time beginning the process of bringing family members through the journey towards a new vision for the Trust's services.

Approaching change

As leaders, change is one of the constants we face, and in the current environment, the pace of change is ever-increasing, demanding more and more of us as we strive to bring our people with us, secure their commitment and participation, and retain their loyalty. It follows, therefore, that being able to lead through change, and communicate that change in a way that is meaningful to those we are asking to follow us, is one of the most important skills a leader needs today and in the future.

One way to break down the requirements of effective change communication is to consider it in three elements – each of which were demonstrated to good effect in the Camphill Village Trust meeting I mentioned above: clarity, collaboration and consistency.

Clarity

In my experience working with many leaders and businesses, it's easy to forget, in the excitement of finally announcing a change that's been planned for months or weeks, that to others it may come as a bombshell. Constructive leadership during periods of change is a process, not an interaction or a single announcement. It requires careful planning, an understanding of the way others might react and, most importantly, as Sara Thakkar demonstrated, a clear-sighted, well-articulated vision for the future.

One of the most widely understood models of understanding human behaviour during change is known as the SCARF model. This was developed by David Rock in 2008 and covers five domains of human social experience: status, certainty, autonomy, relatedness and fairness (Rock, 2008). Essentially, this framework identifies normal threats and stress reward reactions that occur when we're faced with upheaval. This means we as leaders can spot pressure points and take appropriate action.

What I found most interesting when considering this framework in the context of Sara Thakkar's presentation was that every member of the team who joined the discussion was clearly on board with the direction of travel, knew the role that they were expected to play and engaged fully in a lively question-and-answer session. They had autonomy in their responses, came across as a close-knit team and were able to throw the conversational ball to each other with skill and confidence. An excellent example of a team that had been supported, prepared and led through the change process.

Collaboration

True collaboration comes from listening as much as it does from speaking. It comes from setting out the challenges and opportunities of the situation to be faced and fully engaging with the reactions, suggestions and direction from your closest team members.

When my group of health communications agencies was acquired by one of the big media holding companies, we were asked, as part of the deal, to take on the management of a health advertising business that had been struggling for some time. The idea was to bring our leadership and expertise to revitalize what had potential but needed a new focus. Exciting, and just the kind of new challenge we'd been looking for.

What we hadn't anticipated was what this would mean for our existing teams, not least the question of distance. The new business was located on the opposite side of London, which meant spending large amounts of time away from base at a time when the operational changes brought by acquisition were having a huge impact. There was additional pressure from our acquirer to bring everyone together in the same location – a huge upheaval for all the people who had been working with us for years prior to the acquisition. For some, it would add nearly an hour to their commute, and, like every service industry, our business was only as good as our people. Without them, the agencies would fail. We had to find a way to bring everybody together that recognized their competing needs.

In the end, I decided to ask our leadership team within the existing businesses what they thought we should do. I agreed to support whatever decision they made, even though I knew our acquirer had its own desired outcome.

We spent time working together, focused on two simple questions. The first was all about what was best for them as individuals when it came to the pros and cons of relocation. The second question asked them to consider what was best for all the businesses, which were increasingly being asked to work together to solve our clients' problems.

In the end, they voted to move into the single location that had been offered, even though it meant upheavals to their commutes and working patterns, because they believed it was the best way to ensure the continued success of the companies they'd worked so hard to build. Had I insisted on a relocation without consulting the leadership team and genuinely agreeing to support their proposed course of action, I am certain we would have lost people who were crucial to the future of the organization.

The other unexpected advantage of pursuing this course of action was that each member of the leadership team had fully embraced the rationale for the move. They stepped up to become ambassadors across the group, fostering an open dialogue that enabled people to air their concerns, coming up with additional suggestions as to how to make the relocation work.

In hindsight, and viewed through the SCARF lens, we had together been through the whole process, however unwittingly. That collaboration and authentic engagement powered the whole of the relocation, and we retained the majority of our original team even two years post-move.

Consistency

The frequency and consistency of change communication is an important part of organizational transformation. The key is to consider who needs to know what, by when and how the information will be communicated. In the example I shared at the beginning of this chapter, it was clear that a series of audiences and their needs had been identified so that each could be communicated within a planned and consistent fashion. The CEO's team had been thoroughly briefed and were key ambassadors able to show how change was positively impacting the people they support. The next step was to ensure family members also bought into and understood some of the evolution that was taking place, and that kick-off meeting was an important introduction.

One of the differentiators for Camphill Village Trust is that the majority of their communities are in rural locations, so part of what the organization is doing is emphasizing the powerful influence that setting and nature can have in enriching people's lives. The residents of the community where my brother lives have been closely involved in establishing a daily nature walk and sharing photos and videos of the wildlife they spot. As a family member, it was invigorating to share their experiences. During our walk, team members talked eloquently about the way in which the people they supported were benefiting from getting closer to their surroundings. This brought the power of nature absolutely to life and left me feeling even more positive about what Camphill Village Trust is trying to achieve.

How to communicate

Outside of my caring responsibilities, I have spent my professional life advising organizations on how to communicate. Over the years, experience has taught me some straightforward, practical steps to consider when leading others through change, which I thought I would share below.

Thinking about the office relocation mentioned earlier, I reflected on the time I spent simply talking to people above me and alongside me in the organization's hierarchy so they understood my overall objective and how I planned to approach it. This meant I had to work with global HR and finance as well as leaders above me in the pecking order, to secure their agreement before even raising the subject of relocation with my own leadership team. The goal was to ensure smooth, collaborative buy-in to the change proposed, so making sure I'd briefed upwards was critical.

Then, when planning how to communicate beyond my leadership team about the office relocation, it was important to take a step back to simplify the messages I wanted to communicate. To do that, I took a blank piece of paper and worked through the three to five points that got to the absolute heart of what I wanted to say. The discipline of three to five single sentences, written in straightforward 'spoken' language rather than anything official or flowery, forced me to cut to the chase. After testing and refining them with my colleagues, those three to five points formed the basis for every kind of communication. Once they were in place, the hard work really began.

This meant focusing first on my internal leadership teams, encouraging them in turn to fan out to local team leaders and thence through to the wider organization. One of the important decisions we made together was to identify which individuals we wanted to brief very slightly in advance of or alongside announcements. The idea was to look at who were the informal leaders – not in a hierarchical sense but those who had influence within their teams. We described them as social leaders – the people at the cultural heart of the business, if you like.

We also spent some considerable time looking at the potential questions and concerns people might have so we could prepare accordingly by literally asking ourselves those questions and plotting out likely replies. It wasn't about learning answers by rote but more about at least having thought about what we might want to say. Of course, there were questions we hadn't thought about, but I think that simply acknowledging we didn't know the answers and would come back when we'd looked into them added to the integrity of those conversations.

One of the most common missteps I've come across in change communication is to assume that once is enough. Repetition is crucial. In marketing and PR, we often talk about the rule of seven – meaning people need to hear things a minimum of seven times before they retain the information. As human beings, when we are presented with change, especially if it's unexpected, we often don't take in large amounts of the information we're provided with, so timing and frequency of the communications cascade is another critical element of the change communications process.

Consider different routes, too. Perhaps an initial launch meeting, followed by a series of smaller meetings. Email and voice notes, posters, mailers, printed newsletters, short-form video content and instant messaging are all tools that can be used to reinforce the roll-out of communications. People learn and absorb information in very different ways and find their own ways of responding, so it's worth keeping an open mind about the 'how' of communication.

During our acquisition process, alongside announcements, emails and one-to-one and small group meetings, I also ran a regular weekly and then fortnightly blog – Ask Anna. Every member of the company was encouraged to submit questions – some did so anonymously, others came to speak to me personally to alert me to issues that had been raised and others were happy to publicly challenge. It was an opportunity to air concerns, large and small – from whether there would be the same biscuits available in the new office to whether we would provide bursaries for our entry-level staff to help them with their increased travel costs – you name it, people asked, and it was important that I answered.

I can't say for certain what tools Camphill Village Trust, under Sara Thakkar's leadership, used to communicate within their teams, but as a family member, that first meeting kicked off a cascade that continues to this day. My inbox regularly pings with email updates, there are quarterly Family Forums, both online and in person, and I know that the people who live in the communities across the UK are fully engaged in co-creating what their futures look like. And on social channels, I am frequently exposed to videos, photos and other posts highlighting everything from footage of nest boxes across all the communities during the Big Garden Birdwatch for the RSPB, to the talented cheesemakers of Botton Village, beautiful Christmas gifts made by hand at the Larchfield Community and plans for a special 'Festover' weekend at the Delrow Community.

Change is a constant

As leaders, our role is to help people understand why change is important, to communicate clearly, collaboratively and consistently so that they understand the destination and how it is to be achieved. With effective preparation, and a focus on putting yourself in the shoes of your people, that constant of change can be empowering and energizing to everyone involved.

> **REFLECTIONS**
>
> 1. What does the new future you envisage look like in practice – how can you bring that to life for everyone involved?
> 2. Who are your stakeholders, formal and informal?
> 3. Imagine yourself on the receiving end of the change you envision – how would that make you feel? Do you really understand the impact of the changes you're asking people to make?
> 4. How might you need to change course in order to bring people with you on the journey?

Reference

Rock, D. (2008) 'SCARF: A brain-based model for collaborating with and influencing others.' *NeuroLeadership Journal 1*, 7887.

• Chapter 5 •

SUCCESS, FAILURE AND THE TOLL OF LEADERSHIP

Bill Mumford

> Bill Mumford was the CEO of the national charity MacIntyre, the Director of the Government's Improving Lives programme, Non-Executive Director of NICE and Chair of national groups including the Voluntary Organisations Disability Group and National Market Development Forum (Think Local, Act Personal partnership). He was subsequently a hospice CEO, Non-Executive Director of Cumbria Health on Call and Trustee at Skills for Care. He is now retired.

It took me a while to develop my own learning and I am still processing my feelings, which is why I believe sharing one's personal learning is so important...

I have seen too many good people in health and social care who have been burned out or spat out. Good, honest, hardworking, dedicated folk who have spent their career in the service of others. Maybe not flawless but nonetheless driven by a desire to make a positive difference and, far more often than not, they managed to do just that. I too have experienced a bit of burnout and also a feeling of rejection – the latter being the most painful. My learning is mostly this: regardless of the consequences, professional and personal, it will always be 'right' to 'do the right thing', but we need trusted people around us who understand the personal pain of those consequences and who help provide a sense of perspective.

The scandal of the systematic and criminal abuse of people with learning disabilities at Winterbourne View in 2011 ignited such outcry that the public and professional response was: 'No more.'

I felt the same; throughout my career as a social worker and then a social care leader, there had been too many such scandals. During the 1970s, institutional services for people with mental health needs and people with learning disabilities were seen as hotbeds for poor and abusive practice. Since then, a large evidence base has confirmed institutional care as not just correlative but actually contributive, if not causative, to abusive practice (Kamavarapu *et al.*, 2017). This is well known and accepted, so how could such a model of service still be commissioned and regulated 40 years later?

A ministerial-led, cross-sector partnership, the Joint Improvement Programme, was created in 2012 with the expectation that it would bring an end to such institutions and evidence the effectiveness of good community-based, personalized care for all. Despite the early optimism, it was generally agreed after the first year that the partnership was floundering. There was a sense of growing anger from the families and individuals affected by Winterbourne View and a deep frustration was shared by all the partners.

Then, one year later in late 2013, came my 'tap on the shoulder'. I was already in a position of leadership having built up a national learning disability charity with a reputation for quality, progressive thinking and effectiveness. I was also trusted by the partner organizations, including individual self-advocacy groups, family groups and a wide range of influential sector improvement organizations.

The 'tap' was to ask if I might step in and take over the directorship of the Joint Improvement Programme, working to the secretary of state, Norman Lamb, the three sponsoring partners – the Department of Health, NHS England and Local Government Association – and the partnership board.

In the context of austerity policies by the Coalition Government at that time, absolutely no executive authority and virtually no budget, why did I ignore the warnings of trusted colleagues and accept a seemingly 'Mission Impossible'? Why did I take the risk? Was it hubris of leadership, susceptibility to flattery or a perverse pleasure of tilting at windmills?

Before accepting, I spent time meeting with and listening to the Winterbourne families in person. Perhaps then, the desire to help was stronger than the fear of failure.

However, this is not the subject of this chapter. Six months into the role, there was a scandal within my own organization. There was an allegation of abuse perpetrated by my staff against young people with learning disabilities. On receiving the news, my response as a professional was to respond with integrity and do the right thing by resigning. My feeling as an individual was that the ground had opened up beneath my feet.

Colleagues in my organization had reacted quickly with complete integrity, and it soon became clear this had been an isolated, one-off incident. But my high-profile role meant the organization came under intense scrutiny and suspicion, the like of which it had never experienced before.

The eventual outcome was that there was a police and regulator investigation which resulted in no action being taken against the accused staff or MacIntyre. MacIntyre had acted immediately and appropriately on first hearing of the concerns raised by a member of staff. These concerns were not corroborated by anyone else in the investigation nor had there been any prior incidents either reported or unreported found.

I describe myself as a reluctant leader: a person with a strong sense of mission and purpose but little personal ambition. I started my social work career having run away from a blue-chip graduate development programme to work for Barnardo's in a residential school for children with disabilities. I loved the work, really loved it, and I look back on those early formative years as the happiest in my working life. I studied for my social work qualifications at the University of Manchester, where my student placements were within the large institutions known as psychiatric hospitals. The learning was fast and raw at times, but there was excitement in the air with the talk of 'care in the community', which was seen as a radical new direction that could result in the closure of all large, long-stay institutions for people with disabilities and the creation instead of real homes in local communities in which people could build their lives.

Those experiences and the hope for a better way shaped me as a professional social worker and eventually a social care leader. I had developed and continue to have a visceral dislike of institutional models of care.

I don't consider myself to be naïve: poor practice or even abusive practice can and does happen everywhere and in all settings. I'd witnessed this in other colleagues and as a manager had responded to alerts and serious concerns on a number of occasions.

Indeed, before I agreed to take on the directorship of the Joint Improvement Programme, a trusted colleague had warned me that, as the CEO of a large service-providing organization, I needed to be prepared for this. There was every chance a safeguarding issue might arise within my own service, and I needed to know how I would respond.

So maybe I am naïve after all; I thought I did know how I'd respond. My strategy, as much as I had any, was to be managerial, rational and abstract and to compartmentalize the issue. My 'good' integrity would not be conflated with the 'bad' of Winterbourne. I had managed difficult situations before and would do so again.

What I wasn't prepared for was my emotional reaction, which was much more extreme than anything I'd experienced previously.

As planned, my response was managerial, ensuring everything was being done exactly as it should. I took care to ensure I was being immediately transparent with all the partners, speaking with and apologizing to the Winterbourne families, tweeting and blogging updates and offering my immediate resignation from the project, which was accepted.

Privately, however, I felt angry, ashamed and embarrassed with an intensity I'd never felt before. The opportunity and purpose of this role really mattered to me. It was personal. I felt I'd let down the individuals and families of Winterbourne View, I'd let down the minister, I'd let down my sector colleagues who had been so supportive and, at the same time, I'd let down my own organization.

Having left the Joint Improvement Programme, I tried to hide the intensity of my personal feelings while being busy back supporting my own organization. I've never been good at reflecting on and understanding my emotional reactions: better just to set them aside and move on. Be busy, create a new project, run more miles, keep up appearances, learn and move on. None of this did anything to assuage my personal sense of anger and loss.

I was the leader. I'm expected to lead, be positive, provide hope and provide a vision of what good will result. But before long, the personal began to spill over. The frustration was projected onto trusted colleagues. My general tendency to be impatient was experienced by them as intolerance. My normal focus became an obsessional checking, which was experienced as distrust. My high expectations became an unachievable and stress-inducing burden for others to bear.

In short, my empathy was compromised and depleted by my inability to recognize and appropriately deal with my inner turmoil.

Then, after 30 years' service, I was politely asked to leave.

I was depressed. Denial is a strong defence mechanism and I had maxed out on it. However, there's something about night terrors – pounding pulse, breathlessness, 2 a.m. awakening and being afraid to go back to sleep – that's hard to deny! The night terrors were frequent, intense and debilitating. Of course, there was absolutely no thought of seeking medical attention. It will pass and I will move on.

Some colleagues (perhaps those not being battered!) understood this and tried to help. Despite my reluctance, or maybe even my inability to open up, these good colleagues stuck at it. Looking back, they must have been frustrated by my wall of denial. They continued to respond with lots of reassurance, belief, affirmation and perspective while at the same time gently advising caution about how quickly I thought I could bounce back.

I didn't listen, and within just a couple of weeks, I'd run away to the hills and started in a new role as CEO of a joint children and adult hospice in north Cumbria.

A fresh start in a new sector, with new colleagues and new networks. I was still doing something worthwhile, but it was smaller, more connected and reassuringly reminiscent of my earlier career. No one knew or cared about my former roles. At first it worked. I was smiling, engaging and enjoying the new challenge. There was lots of new learning and an important job to be done.

But the night terrors continued. I've always been a keen runner but my running was curtailed by an injury that couldn't be fixed, and to make matters worse, the injury was preventing my escape to the hills.

Depression started to take over again. This time, I had the insight to know it was my issue and my issue alone. After just two years in the post, I stood down. My self-belief was in tatters. Fortunately, my supportive colleagues continued with their affirmation and I was by now more receptive to their advice. I needed a pause, a proper 'down-tools' reflective reset. I listened to the people I trusted most and with their help started to build more insight into the triggers of my continued vulnerabilities.

Having spoken to several colleagues with similarly traumatic work experiences, it's been interesting to learn the various ways that they went about restoring their mental wellbeing. The one thing they all had in common was: it takes time. More time than we might think and wish.

Using the simple Five Ways to Wellbeing framework below (Aked *et al*., 2008), I created a personal plan that helped me to rebalance by focusing on those areas where I struggle the most.

- Being active.
- Taking time to be present.
- Building deeper connections with others.
- Developing my learning.
- Giving back.

I like a cognitive framework; for me, it provides a good starting point and a structure that I find helpful for communicating both to myself and others as well as for self-reflection.

For example, being overly focused on one of the five ways – being active – was not working. In fact, because of my running injury, it was making things worse as I neglected other areas that were equally important.

My initial plan took 20 minutes while sitting in a café with a coffee and slice of chocolate tiffin. I shared it with loved ones and friends (I include my supportive colleagues in this small trusted group). I believe this was the first time I'd been able to be truly open about how I felt. Use of this simple tool helped me admit feelings that I hadn't been able to acknowledge before.

As many will testify, healing takes time. This was a beginning – a first step but not a conclusion. With the help and understanding of others, I still have to keep at it. Over time, the night terrors diminished and were less frightening. My recalling and re-enacting of difficult conversations lessened and started being replaced by softer and more positive memories. I've changed the way I now earn a living and am happy to be able to still make a positive contribution.

Do I find it hard to look back on my career and remember the good times? Yes. Do I still have a deep nagging sense of failure? Yes. Do I feel that what I have created since is not as fulfilling as what could have been? Yes. However, the anger has gone and I've no sense of grievance. There's no self-pity, just a loss of purpose. A loss that eases with time, better balance and the continuation of having good people around me.

I should like to conclude my own experience by making a wider observation. Essential personal accountability comes at significant cost to senior leaders in the public sector but there's also a risk of cost to the sector in the loss of experienced leaders who have made and could still make a significant and positive contribution. These might be people who have taken on responsible roles for what we believe to be the right reasons: public service, a sincere desire to make a difference and an ability to provide hope in a counsel of despair.

Could more be done to help senior leaders who go through difficult times before it's too late for them personally? Perhaps we expect the impossible of our senior leaders; the depth of need within our society and the complexity and cost of addressing this are just too difficult to resolve, so knocking leaders off their chargers may provide a helpful distraction from the unpalatable reality of the impossibility of their role.

Leadership comes with responsibility and accountability. Each individual interprets this in different ways, and for me, a strong sense of responsibility and accountability has always come naturally.

For example, take the curious incident of the school Christmas tree, something I am remembered for over 50 years later. Said tree was discovered on the roof of the headteacher's office having been taken, fully decorated, from the assembly hall, and no one saw me do it. I fessed up and narrowly escaped expulsion. My only regret was that I never did manage to get the lights to work.

More seriously, I didn't hesitate to offer my resignation from the Joint Improvement Programme, nor did I offer any resistance to being asked to leave my own organization. I can only lead with a sense of consensus. Many others do the same: we need to bear this in mind when the immediate reaction to a serious concern is to seek the resignation of the person in charge so the organization can move on. Where exactly they are hoping to move on to is often not clear!

It would be hubris for me to suggest that either former employer suffered a setback with my leaving, as the reality is that they and the sector as a whole continues to grind on regardless. For the ground-down individual, it feels very personal but it isn't. Few in the public sector will be pleased to see someone take a fall, but for most it is just like passing an accident on the motorway, a momentary reminder to slow down before we speed up again.

This impersonal response is for the most part not a conscious lack of care, but it may be a subconscious sector displacement where frustration and lack of agency of workers within a grinding system are redirected onto our leaders who can't match our expectations and let us down.

Personally, I believe such nihilism needs to be countered by those leaders who continue to breathe some oxygen into a dark and airless sector, providing hope to those colleagues who continue to light candles.

There is extensive research on reducing executive burnout and there are lots of 'top tips' for successful leaders. If something works for you then use it. I have only two suggestions.

First, for councillors, trustees and board members, to prioritize taking independent advice on how best to look after their leadership teams, and to create a more enlightened plan than the typical business-continuity, reputational-damage-limitation approach so frequently adopted.

Second, for leaders to be actively encouraged to build a network of trusted support and formal mentoring to help understand and avoid the fallacy of the hero leader.

> **REFLECTIONS**
>
> 1. Who can you trust and share your personal doubt, anger, sadness and deep insecurities with?
> 2. Who do you value for giving you an honest and objective opinion while still feeling safe?
> 3. Who will help you rediscover and sustain self-worth and perspective?

References

Aked, J., Marks, N., Cordon, C. and Thompson, S. (2008) *Five Ways to Wellbeing: Communicating the Evidence*. London: New Economics Foundation. https://neweconomics.org/2008/10/five-ways-to-wellbeing

Kamavarapu, Y. S., Ferriter, M., Morton, S. and Völlm, B. (2017) 'Institutional abuse – Characteristics of victims, perpetrators and organisations: A systematic review.' *European Psychiatry 40*, 45–54.

• Chapter 6 •

SOCIAL INFLUENCE AND BUTTERFLY EFFECTS

Michael Sanders and Vanessa Hirneis

> Michael Sanders is a professor of public policy, Director of the School for Government and Director of the Policy Institute's Experimental Government Team at King's College London. His work focuses on the use of causal methods and particularly randomized trials to evaluate policy interventions, the use of behavioural science in policy design and increasing social mobility and opportunity. He has previously served as the Founding Chief Executive of What Works for Children's Social Care and Chief Scientist at the Behavioural Insights Team.

> Vanessa Hirneis is a social psychologist for the Policy Institute's Experimental Government Team at King's College London. Her work focuses on evidence-based and behaviourally informed policy to improve outcomes for marginalized groups. Previously, Vanessa worked in various 'nudge' units including at the World Bank, the Behavioural Insights Team and Innovations for Poverty Action.

Much of the academic literature on leadership focuses on the power of leadership to effect change and consequently centres on the role of the individual leader. This makes sense – to the extent that a leader is the most important single individual in an endeavour and given the focus (particularly in the West) on the single charismatic visionary as a driver of change.

However, there is a large and growing literature on the power of social connectedness, belongingness, comparison and norms, which shows that the behaviour of others around you – and particularly those whom you consider to be close peers – strongly influences your own behaviour in work and in life.

In this chapter, we explore what researchers can tell us about the power of social influence and how it can be used by organizations and their leaders to bring about meaningful and lasting change.

Butterfly effects in leadership

Leaders are powerful – there can be no doubt about that. The leader of a team, or an organization, is usually (if not always) the more influential person in the organization.

They have the bulk of the organization's 'hard power' – they can make the rules, choose whom and what to reward, choose whom to sanction and set the direction of an organization.

But they also shape the 'soft power' within an organization – the culture, the mood music, the acceptable norms. It is easy to overlook the importance of this soft power when we are considering how best to be leaders, and to place too much of a focus on the role of strategy, direction-setting and inspiration from the top.

But culture, as is often said, eats strategy for breakfast. Consider the metaphor of a river and a rock. The rock is strong and unyielding but is gradually worn down by the persistent, constant power of the river; so culture erodes the rules and the stated intentions of leaders, one inch at a time. The rock in the path of our raft shapes our immediate future, but it is the river that decides, in the end, where we are headed.

While we should not overstate the role of hard power, we should also not overstate the relative soft power of leaders compared with others in the organization. The director, perhaps ensconced behind the walls of their office and in back-to-back meetings all day, might have less influence on their subordinates' mood than the receptionist who greets everyone every morning.

Even the ebb and flow of influence within an organization – who's in and who's out of the inner circle – can be more effectively controlled by the director's PA (personal assistant) than by the leader themselves – as the PA can choose who gets a meeting with the boss and when. The power to change organizations is also often diffuse and hard to predict. Just as the flap of a butterfly's wing causes a storm a thousand miles away, small interactions can shape the future of organizations.

In this chapter, we consider the role of the social features of a team or an organization and how they influence the behaviour and performance of individuals and the unit itself. We'll consider how these features might be influenced by leaders looking to harness the power of social influence and how leaders' own behaviours can shape outcomes in ways that they might not intend.

Norms

One of the most widely known findings in behavioural science is that people are strongly influenced by social norms. A social norm is the sense, either implicit or explicit, of what most people do (a 'descriptive' norm) or what most people think is the right thing to do (an 'injunctive' norm). For example, in London, there is a strong descriptive norm around standing on the right-hand side of escalators to keep the left-hand side free for people in a hurry. This is a behaviour we infer from observing others, and we follow suit to maintain order. On the other hand, there is also a strong injunctive norm in most workplaces against putting your feet up on the desk – we don't necessarily see others doing it, but we implicitly know that it would go against the social expectation of professionalism.

Some norms are more salient than others, and leaders can influence others by acknowledging and promoting particular norms to encourage behaviours, which can be particularly effective when people tend to underestimate the prevalence of a positive behaviour.

Perhaps the most famous study of descriptive social norms was conducted by Michael Hallsworth and colleagues (2017). They worked with the UK Government's tax authority, HMRC, to try to increase tax repayment by people who were late in paying their taxes. To do this, they added a sentence to the top of letters informing people that 'Nine out of ten people in the UK pay their tax on time. You are currently in the very small minority of people who have not paid us yet.' Doing so had the effect of significantly increasing the rate at which people filled in their tax returns and made their tax payments – bringing forward some £200 million in tax revenue.

Within organizations, social norms are often hidden. We might *think* that most people do not comply with particular rules or regulations, which will likely influence us to not do so ourselves, when actually compliance is very high – for example, with the organization's expenses policy or room-booking system. Surfacing positive social norms can be very powerful in helping to change people's behaviour to be in line with these norms.

Some norms are not stated but can be found in our physical environment. In the Netherlands, Kees Keizer, a researcher in environmental psychology, and colleagues located a tidy alley in a shopping area where people often parked their bikes. They attached flyers for a non-existent store to the bikes and watched people's behaviour. Next, they did the same thing after spraying graffiti on the walls of the alley and making it untidy. When there was rubbish all around (a norm of messiness), people were more likely to cast the flyer from their bike onto the street, while they were more likely to put it in a bin or take it with them if the area was generally tidy (a norm of tidiness). They also found that if it was untidy but there was someone in the process of tidying it (like a street sweeper), this also decreased the rate of littering (Keizer, Lindenberg and Steg, 2008).

We should also be cautious of the power that leaders have to make and shape norms in negative ways. In one organization that we worked with, there was an official policy of everyone hotdesking and much talk of a 'flat, non-hierarchical structure'.

In practice, the managing director always sat at the same desk, which had an impressive collection of his shoes underneath and his rain jacket more or less living on the back of his chair. This simple act showed the staff that no matter what the official line was, there was a hierarchy and not *everyone* had to hotdesk. They might have been happier if the policy had exempted the senior staff from hotdesking – instead of the policy saying one thing but the norm being another.

Competition

Sometimes a bit of healthy competition in the workplace can make a difference to our performance, as long as the competition is structured in a way that is positive. We want to ensure that people feel part of the whole and that teams are not rivalrous with one another.

We tried this successfully in an experiment to boost physical activities with employees of a large employer in the construction sector. All participants were given Fitbit fitness trackers. After a month of wearing them, we asked them to take part in a competition to increase their physical activity (in this case, step counts) measured by the devices.

Rather than competing as individuals, participants competed in their teams. So if you and I were teammates, your performance would support our team; I have an incentive to increase not just my own step count but yours too, cementing the bonds between team members. Teams were sorted into 'leagues' of five teams based on the number of steps measured in the month prior to the competition starting – this meant that nobody faced an insurmountable struggle and every team had a chance of winning their league.

Every week during the challenge, we provided one group of the teams with information about their performance (average number of steps per day). For the second group of teams, we provided richer social information about the league, such as which team was ahead in the league and how big their lead was in steps, as well as giving step counts for the chasing teams – creating a more salient social comparison.

At the end of the month, we saw a 10% increase in physical activity by people in the second group of teams compared with the first group – the social information motivated an average increase of 800 steps per day. The increases were largest for people in the middle of the league – who had both someone behind them to fear and someone ahead of them to aspire to beat – and less so for teams at the top or bottom of each league.

In another experiment, we tested making social comparisons with yourself – giving people a target of either 10,000 steps per day (the default setting for Fitbits) or beating their prior step count by 10%, which increased each week as their step count rose.

For many people, and particularly those who were very close to or even above the 10,000 steps per day count, the static target wasn't motivating, but the dynamic, personalized target increased the step count significantly.

These experiments show how, if used sparingly, initiatives to collaborate with others towards a common goal or to compete with oneself in fun and gamified ways can be great tools to keep people engaged and motivated.

Recognition and wellbeing

Helping people to feel recognized for their work can make a difference to their wellbeing and motivation. Pay has obvious benefits, but when working in the public sector, it can often be hard to find the money to offer meaningful pay rises – especially during a time of austerity. Similarly, reducing caseloads might have a big effect on wellbeing but is not within the gift of most managers.

There is also some evidence that small cash incentives might not be terribly effective – or at least, that we should be careful about how we make use of them. Research by Elizabeth Dunn, Lara Aknin and Michael Norton (2008), three social psychologists, shows that small cash bonuses can be more effective at improving wellbeing and productivity when they're set up in a prosocial way.

In one study, they randomized people into three conditions – to receive no financial bonus, to receive a small bonus of $20 to spend on themselves or to receive the same sized bonus with the caveat that it had to be spent on someone else. They then monitored people's wellbeing and found that they were happier if they spent the money on someone else than if they had spent it on themselves.

In a follow-up study in a call centre, they tried the same thing with people responsible for making sales over the telephone and found that people who received the bonus to spend on someone else were significantly more productive than those given money to spend on themselves.

There is also value in showing people recognition in non-financial ways. Jana Gallus (2017), a behavioural economist at UCLA, conducted an experiment with Wikipedia editors (who volunteer their time to write, update and edit the free online encyclopaedia) in which some received a 'symbolic recognition' – a badge on their Wikipedia profile – to recognize their contribution. She found that editors who received the symbolic recognition went on to contribute more.

Similarly, Adam Grant (2008) found that when university fundraisers received thanks and recognition from a scholarship recipient, they went on to be more productive compared with people who hadn't received thanks.

We tested the potential of symbolic recognition with social workers in England (O'Flaherty, Sanders and Whillans, 2021). Some teams received letters from a senior leader in the local authority to thank them for their work, containing specific positive feedback from their team manager. We found that this reduced burnout and increased the wellbeing of the social workers who received the intervention.

Taken together, these findings from research suggest that there are ways of showing recognition and supporting people's wellbeing without spending huge amounts of money.

Diversity

Diversity makes organizations thrive, but to achieve a diverse workforce, it is not enough to focus efforts solely on hiring from a more diverse pool of people.

In fact, the true challenge may lie in managing diverse teams successfully, including managing expectations of what this looks like.

A group or organization can be considered diverse when its members are heterogenous across gender, ethnicity, age, sexual orientation, cultural and other social identity categories. We want to promote such diversity in organizations because it is the right thing to do and because, luckily in this case, the right thing also rewards us from an economic standpoint. Researchers have long found that diversity makes for better outcomes because diverse teams are more innovative, are more creative and make smarter choices (Mannix and Neale, 2005; Yang, Tian and Woodruff, 2022).

But this is only half the story. When comparing decision outcomes of teams joined by a socially similar (homogenous) and a socially dissimilar (heterogenous) newcomer, Katherine W. Phillips and colleagues (2009) found that diverse teams consistently outperformed those that were not diverse. However, when asked questions about the team's confidence in their results or their level of comfort throughout the decision-making process, diverse teams indicated lower levels of confidence in their answers and that their interactions were less effective.

In fact, there is a considerably large body of research suggesting that group diversity can lead to more difficult interactions, more conflict, more discomfort and less trust (Galinsky *et al.*, 2015; Van Knippenberg and Mell, 2016).

We need to be diligent about addressing existing biases towards individuals or groups whose demographic backgrounds are different to our own, as these biases will have important real-life implications for others, for us and for the health of the organization as a whole.

Robert B. Lount and colleagues (2015) investigated such bias towards diverse teams. The researchers recruited working professionals who were enrolled on a part-time MBA programme in the US and had them read through and watch team interactions while asking them to rate the team's level of relationship conflict. Everyone read and watched the same interactions but, at random, some participants were given clues that the team they observed was racially diverse while others were told it was racially homogenous. Their research found that participants wrongfully perceived diverse teams to demonstrate more relationship conflict and that, as a consequence, observing participants were less willing to allocate additional financial resources to such teams compared with those that were racially homogenous.

Where there is an abundance of different social identities, backgrounds, perspectives and cultural norms coming together, there is bound to also be a certain degree of tension. Yet, tension – despite the often negative connotations of the word – does not need to be a bad thing; it simply needs to be managed.

Organizations can manage this tension and promote inclusion by implementing effective Equity, Diversity and Inclusion (EDI) processes. This includes but is not limited to the integration of clearly defined EDI goals into the company's mission (e.g., setting measurable targets to improve representation of underrepresented groups), the implementation of adequate (e.g., contextualized) recruitment and hiring practices, ongoing training and awareness programmes, the creation of safe spaces for dialogue and the establishment of anonymous feedback systems, dedicated diversity officers and/or conflict resolution processes. People of different backgrounds need to feel included in the whole of the organization and to feel supported and safe to express themselves when things are not going well. Bias needs to be unveiled and addressed, and uncomfortable conversations need to be had consistently and in a way that ensures empathy and accountability.

Simply put, to reap the benefits of diversity, leaders need to put in effort. Representation is great but inclusion will always be better – for everyone.

Network nudges

This chapter has thus far focused on the power of leaders to influence others. However, there are likely to be many occasions when leaders themselves are not the best messengers to encourage a particular set of behaviours.

For example, the real or perceived social distance between messengers and those expected to act has been shown to make a difference to the power of behaviour change. We see this in an experiment we carried out in 2012, with a large investment bank in London (Behavioural Insights Team, 2013). In this study, participants were randomly assigned to receive an email encouraging them to make a donation to charity.

The emails came from the CEO and were identical save for the fact that half were addressed to 'Dear colleague' while the others were to 'Dear John' (or whatever the recipient's first name was).

This was a small change with a big effect – the proportion of people donating rose from 2% when the email was sent to 'Dear colleague' to 8% when it was made more personal. What was most interesting, however, is *who* was most affected by the intervention. This followed a pattern: the more senior someone was, the more likely they were (in general) to respond positively to the treatment.

There are a couple of possible explanations for this, but our experiment wasn't designed to determine motivations. One explanation that appealed to us related to social distance – the idea that the closer you are to someone socially, the more influential they are in your decisions. For example, Gary Charness and Uri Gneezy (2008) found that people are more likely to behave prosocially when they know the name of the person who benefits compared with when they are anonymous.

To test this theory further, we developed a series of 'network nudges' – whereby instead of nudging an individual in a high position (like via a CEO email), we nudge someone who is socially closer to them and ask them to change the behaviour of their network (Behavioural Insights Team, 2016).

Across two further experiments, we observed substantially more influence being generated by featuring the names of people who are socially closer to the recipient. For example, we worked with a large employer to try and boost enrolment in workplace training. With one business unit, we invited everyone in the unit to take part in training that would result in a maths qualification. With the second business unit, we invited people who had taken the course before to encourage others from the same unit to take part. This resulted in a doubling of sign-up rates in the second business unit compared with the first – so more people got to take the training, which would benefit both them (by giving them a maths qualification they would otherwise have lacked) and their employer (by having a more numerate workforce).

Applying this same principle to the original example of charitable fundraising above, we emailed some middle managers who had previously donated and asked them to encourage their colleagues to donate. For other middle managers, we either didn't email them at all or emailed to thank them for their prior donations. The effects were striking – rising from around 5% of people donating to 17% donating when their manager had been *asked* to encourage them to do so – a powerful effect that raised millions of pounds for the chosen charities.

Closing remarks

When thinking about leadership, we often find ourselves fixated on the overt power wielded by leaders – the ability to set rules, direct the course and command from the top. But as we have seen, there are more subtle forces at play: elusive currents of culture, norms and social dynamics that can quietly shape the journey in ways that are easy to overlook. As social animals, it does not come as a surprise that many, if not all, of the things that affect us in our everyday life will also shape our professional ones.

From this perspective, good leadership really is about the building and maintaining of respectful and authentic relationships within the organization as well as about creating the environment for this to become the standard on all levels.

Every good relationship requires work. As we have explored in this chapter, healthy relationships in the workplace require a good reading of explicit and implicit norms, they allow us to grow through cooperative and well-structured challenges and team-based competition and they are nourished through showing appreciation and recognition. Some of our most rewarding and impactful relationships can be with people who broaden our horizons because they are different from us. We can also be aware of the power of social proximity and influence.

Leadership is about more than giving orders, it is about orchestrating the hidden social currents that shape the organizational journey. If you have made it this far, we hope we have managed to illustrate that. In the delicate interplay between leaders and the social fabric, subtle gestures can become agents of substantial change.

> **REFLECTIONS**
> As a leader, or as an aspiring one, we hope you will carry the following questions with you:
>
> 1. What are the written and unwritten rules in my organization and in what ways do they differ?
> 2. Am I encouraging cooperation towards a common goal, or am I unintentionally pitting people against each other?
> 3. What am I doing to recognize people's effort, work and value? How can I do more?

4. Am I making space for people of all backgrounds, beliefs and experiences? Am I actively building a team that can withstand temporary discomfort as a means to achieve an inclusive environment?
5. Who are the most powerful messengers in my organization, and how can I create more closeness between team members?

References

Behavioural Insights Team (2013) *Applying Behavioural Insights to Charitable Giving.* www.bi.team/publications/applying-behavioural-insights-to-charitable-giving

Behavioural Insights Team (2016) *Update Report: 2015–16.* www.bi.team/wp-content/uploads/2016/09/BIT_Update_Report_2015-16-.pdf

Charness, G. and Gneezy, U. (2008) 'What's in a name? Anonymity and social distance in dictator and ultimatum games.' *Journal of Economic Behavior and Organization 68*, 1, 29–35.

Dunn, E. W., Aknin, L. B. and Norton, M. I. (2008) 'Spending money on others promotes happiness.' *Science 319*, 5870, 1687–1688.

Galinsky, A. D., Todd, A. R., Homan, A. C., Phillips, K. W., et al. (2015) 'Maximizing the gains and minimizing the pains of diversity: A policy perspective.' *Perspectives on Psychological Science 10*, 6, 742–748.

Gallus, J. (2017) 'Fostering public good contributions with symbolic awards: A large-scale natural field experiment at Wikipedia.' *Management Science 63*, 12, 3999–4015.

Grant, A. M. (2008) 'The significance of task significance: Job performance effects, relational mechanisms, and boundary conditions.' *Journal of Applied Psychology 93*, 1, 108.

Hallsworth, M., List, J. A., Metcalfe, R. D. and Vlaev, I. (2017) 'The behavioralist as tax collector: Using natural field experiments to enhance tax compliance.' *Journal of Public Economics 148*, 14–31.

Keizer, K., Lindenberg, S. and Steg, L. (2008) 'The spreading of disorder.' *Science 322*, 5908, 1681–1685.

Lount, R. B., Sheldon, O. J., Rink, F. and Phillips, K. W. (2015) 'Biased perceptions of racially diverse teams and their consequences for resource support.' *Organization Science 26*, 5, 1351–1364.

Mannix, E. and Neale, M. A. (2005) 'What differences make a difference? The promise and reality of diverse teams in organizations.' *Psychological Science in the Public Interest 6*, 2, 31–55.

O'Flaherty, S., Sanders, M. T. and Whillans, A. (2021) 'Research: A little recognition can provide a big morale boost.' *Harvard Business Review.* https://hbr.org/2021/03/research-a-little-recognition-can-provide-a-big-morale-boost

Phillips, K. W., Liljenquist, K. A. and Neale, M. A. (2009) 'Is the pain worth the gain? The advantages and liabilities of agreeing with socially distinct newcomers.' *Personality and Social Psychology Bulletin 35*, 3, 336–350.

Van Knippenberg, D. and Mell, J. N. (2016) 'Past, present, and potential future of team diversity research: From compositional diversity to emergent diversity.' *Organizational Behavior and Human Decision Processes 136*, 135–145.

Yang, Y., Tian, T. Y. and Woodruff, T. K. (2022) 'Gender-diverse teams produce more novel and higher-impact scientific ideas.' *Proceedings of the National Academy of Sciences 119*, 36, E2200841119.

• Chapter 7 •

EMOTIONAL CULTURE AND LEADERSHIP

Thinking about Emotions, Fear and Anxiety in the Workplace

Peter Buzzi and Claudia Megele

For chapter author biographies, see Chapter 2.

Hardly a day goes by that we don't encounter a struggle with emotions at work. A colleague attempting to hide his or her feelings of frustration; a director angry about the lack of progress in a project; a practitioner who feels anxious about a conflict. While we may extol the power of emotions, we may not always harness that power or be explicit and intentional about the emotional culture we promote.

This chapter reflects on the role of emotions, vulnerability and fear and some of their implications for leadership.

We use the pronoun 'I' when an experience or event relates to one of the authors only.

Leadership and a dehumanized workplace

In his book *Economy and Society*, Max Weber states:

> Bureaucracy develops the more perfectly, the more it is 'dehumanized,' the more completely it succeeds in eliminating from official business love, hatred, and all purely personal, irrational, and emotional elements which escape calculation. This is appraised as its special virtue by capitalism. (Weber, 1978, p.975)

We have come a long way since Weber, although still, for some, the myth of the 'tough and confident leader' collides with the idea of showing emotions and vulnerability in the workplace. We are experiencing an 'emotional revolution' in which meditation and emotional wellbeing are the buzzwords of the C-level executives, and 'alpha' males and females proclaim the virtues of Zen and mindfulness. However, we still remain uncertain about what to do with emotions in the workplace.

Emotions as information

Emotions are deep level signals about information that demand attention (Siegal, 1999). Our appraisal of such signals leads to the meaning of the situation as we perceive it. Therefore, emotions can be thought of as information and are often a trigger for action and/or mood. So emotions offer a window into our own and others' worlds; they tell a story about people and their environment.

Emotions also serve as social signals (Barrett and Nelson-Goens, 1997; Morris and Keltner, 2000). It can be said that our display of emotions is directed at others with the intention to elicit specific behaviour. For example, leaders showing sadness may aim to draw empathy and social support.

Our emotions can influence others through contagion, interpretation or inference. For example, display of sadness may evoke similar emotions in others. While by interpreting our emotion, others may respond to our emotions with a different, complementary and situationally appropriate emotion. For example, a display of anger or irritation by a leader may evoke frustration, discomfort, worry, anxiety or fear in others.

Humans often make inferences and will attribute characteristics or values to others' emotions and behaviours based on their own observations and experience. For example, a leader displaying anger may be presumed to be short-tempered; there may be an inference that they have been offended or failed in some way or perhaps that they are responding to being disobeyed. People may also attribute power, anxiety or weakness to a leader's angry behaviour.

Our reactions, interpretations, assumptions and attributions to a given emotion may differ from others due to our own previous experience and understanding of that emotion. Hence, knowledge of someone's emotions can lead others to assume knowledge of other things; this extends the meaning of emotion and offers additional information, inferred about the person beyond the knowledge of how they are feeling. For example, we make moral and even legal judgements based on inferences about the remorse or guilt in other people.

The display of emotions by leaders affects others' assumptions and appraisals of the leaders' status, power and social influence.

Emotions as a 'thing' to manage

In 1995 Daniel Goleman's bestselling book *Emotional Intelligence: Why It Can Matter More Than IQ* reframed emotions as a set of skills that could be learnt and could contribute to organizational performance.

However, most of the research and discussions about emotions in the workplace are focused on the *individual* as the source and target of emotions. This ignores the systemic nature of human experience and simplifies emotions to some 'thing' we have rather than a reflection of who we are; thinking of emotions as a 'thing' makes them more controllable, more manageable and even 'actionable'. Emotions then become something that can be categorized as a threat or liability and repressed through discipline or an asset that can be harnessed with strategic and operational machinations.

This is exemplified in a conversation I had with the HR department of a public sector organization a few years ago. The organization was on an improvement journey and had experienced significant changes that had led to increasing anxiety, mental health difficulties, long-term illness, burnout and turnover of staff. The director had reached out and asked whether I could offer support groups to staff who were experiencing 'burnout' and resilience training for the leadership team and others. In discussing the scope of the work, the HR director mentioned, 'That's all perfect, but can we make sure every support group meeting also has clear actionable outcomes?'

There seemed to be a gap between the leadership's declared intentions and actions. I thought the HR director's statement could be reflective of organizational culture and more significant systemic challenges.

The organization and its members were overwhelmed with actions and yet the response to their stress was to demand more actions – actions to 'fix' the emotions, actions to mend the 'thing' that was out of balance, the 'thing' that blocked doing the doing. This was epitomized by the fact that every meeting or conversation needed to have actions as its outcome, and the response to every risk was yet another action list; even staff supervision was consumed by checking on actions and agreeing on more actions. Having clear objectives and an actionable plan to achieve those objectives is fundamental to every organization, but for actions to be meaningful, they should be accompanied with thinking and balanced with reflection.

A singular and narrow focus on action can be understood as a defence against the anxiety of thinking. This is particularly evident in emotionally charged environments and risk-laden and anxious organizations where a preoccupation with 'doing' is at the heart of 'busy-ness' and serves as a respite from thinking. However, in the absence of thinking and reflection, the 'busy-ness' of 'doing' and the rush of 'fixing the problem' can result in losing sight of the underlying organizational and emotional culture and systemic challenges. In doing so, we can contribute to and perpetuate the 'problem'. In this case example, people and their emotions were lost in 'action' and were denied the opportunity for thinking and being.

More importantly, we suggest that the denial of emotions and the opportunity for thinking and reflection is a denial of being. The denial of emotions and the space for thinking with a narrow focus on actions and doing is a denial of people's existence as whole persons and reduces people to their labour. This is the essence of commodification of the worker and labour that was born of the industrial revolution. People had always 'worked' in one way or another, but their work was not embedded in a complex system that turned work into a market good. However, the industrial capitalism transformed work – what we do with our bodies and minds and the product of our effort and exertion – into labour – a market commodity with a price (wages). This commodification of work into labour – as a series of tasks and actions with a focus on 'doing' – was a denial of being – a denial of acknowledging the worker as a whole person beyond their labour – and alienating for workers – reducing the worker to a cog in the economic engine of society. This is at the heart of Karl Marx's ideas about alienation of labour as described in his *Economic and Philosophic Manuscripts of 1844* (Marx, 1978, p.74):

> the fact that labour is external to the worker, i.e., it does not belong to his intrinsic nature; that in his work, therefore, he does not affirm himself but denies himself, does not feel content but unhappy, does not develop freely his physical and mental energy but mortifies his body and ruins his mind. The worker therefore only feels himself outside his work, and in his work feels outside himself.

These challenges are often further complicated by the meaning of the work and the urgency of work in health and social care.

The nature of urgent work places urgent demand on our resources, activating the adrenaline axis. This can be exciting, but not necessarily entertaining or helpful. Adrenaline can suppress pain, fear, fatigue, anxiety and thought. Continued experience of an adrenaline rush can be addictive.

In health and social care, this addictive nature of work can be conflated with, and exacerbated by, the embedded value and meaning of the work – contributing to and making a positive impact in other people's lives. Playing the 'busy rescuer' and 'hero' in ('hero-in') difficult situations can be a powerful psychological drug that distracts attention from self, pain and self-anxiety but eventually takes its toll and leads to exhaustion and burnout.

Indeed, 'doing the doing' can be such a powerful 'drug' that the act of slowing down enough to reflect, or even the thought of slow thinking, might be experienced as disturbing.

How many times have we seen such a dynamic play out in health and social care as a consequence of a 'never event' or a serious incident? There might be a rush to bring in an improvement plan or a deadline to introduce a reform-and-reorganization programme, but without reflection, this can result in repeated cycles of action without sufficient learning – and therefore little improvement in outcomes.

Authentic display of emotions and vulnerability

Even in organizations with a flat structure and lateral leadership, power differentials exist. A power dynamic is inherent in every relationship, and power and identity mediate the experience and display of emotions and vulnerability.

Because of this, certain emotions are often associated with and observable in certain positions rather than others. Consider which of the following you'd expect to see in a leader.

- Hope or despair?
- Confidence or hesitance?
- Pride or shame?
- Composure or agitation?
- Vitality or lethargy?
- Flexibility or routine?
- Choice or ambivalence?
- Assertiveness or acquiescence?
- Excitement or exhaustion?

- Enthusiasm or indifference?
- Vocal outrage or silent withdrawal?
- Visibility or invisibility?

The first emotion in each pair is usually associated with, and expected of, people in positions of power, while the second emotion in each pair is associated with people in less powerful and less visible roles.

In this sense, emotions and emotional expressions offer a window into the distribution of power and sense of empowerment. People who feel empowered are more authentic with their display of emotions and feel more at ease with showing emotion at work. On the other hand, people who feel disempowered tend to hide or censor their emotions. This can result in a loss of authenticity and presentation of a 'false identity'.

Leaders' authentic displays of emotions and vulnerability offer others the opportunity to do the same.

We can learn and develop our capacity to be authentic and share our vulnerability, but thinking of emotions and vulnerability purely as a 'skill' distorts their meaning and significance. We have written in greater detail about vulnerability in Chapter 2 of this book. Being vulnerable is about sharing the authentic part of ourselves that we may have otherwise chosen to hide or keep private. Therefore, showing vulnerability is a personal choice, rather than a skill, that requires the self-awareness to ask: Will being open and honest in this moment serve me? Will it serve others?

Being vulnerable with appropriate boundaries can breed trust and stronger connection; however, oversharing and vulnerability without boundaries can be damaging. Hence, many leaders wonder where the limit is and when sharing vulnerability might become oversharing.

To maintain a culture of vulnerability with healthy boundaries and without oversharing, it is helpful to consider whether what we're sharing creates any emotional labour for us or others. If yes, then we may be oversharing and may want to redraw boundaries and reconsider what we're sharing until the answer is no.

Thinking about emotional culture and what makes people tick

Every organization has an emotional culture even if it's an unspoken one of denial and suppression. However, unexpressed and unacknowledged emotions never die; they are buried alive and usually come forth later in uglier ways.

In fact, there are no emotions that we show more than the ones we try to hide. How we show emotions and which emotions we show influence and shape the emotional culture in our organizations, while the emotions that we suppress might find expression with others who share the same feelings and result in subcultures within the organization. This is particularly evident in organizations with rigid hierarchies where staff feel alienated and unacknowledged.

Organizational culture is like a river whose current and direction determine the course of the organization and its destination – where it can go – while subcultures are currents within the organizational current that can distract, disrupt and even sink the organization.

All leaders can describe the cognitive culture of their organization, i.e., shared intellectual values, norms, assumptions and expectations that define how employees should think and behave and serve as a guide for the organization.

However, not every leader can describe and be aware of the emotional culture in their organization.

The following experience demonstrates the difference and some of the implications of the discrepancy between cognitive and emotional cultures.

A few years ago, I was invited to speak at the annual conference of a public sector organization, and my talk was scheduled after the director's welcome message and presentation.

During her presentation, the director asked for conference participants' live feedback about one of the services/departments within the organization where they had introduced a series of changes and 'improvements'. The participants used their mobile phones to provide feedback and the feedback was projected in real time on the screen behind the director. The participants' feedback was totally outstanding.

However, as the glowing feedback and all the praise, applause and heart emojis flooded the screen, what became increasingly more evident was the conspicuous absence of any critical or constructive comments about the service/department in question. During the coffee break, the director told me, 'I was worried about how we're doing but am glad that went well.'

The following year, subsequent to an Ofsted inspection, the organization received a rating of 'requires improvement' for leadership and the service in question.

The practitioners and managers from the service in question who were participating in the conference were intimately familiar with the service's strengths and areas for improvement and yet they didn't provide any constructive suggestions or mention any challenges within the service. Given their intimate knowledge of the dynamics and challenges of their service, they were best positioned to suggest improvements that could make a difference. Perhaps, if they had shared their insight with the director, she could have addressed some of the difficulties or put a plan in place to address the areas of improvement. At the very least, this would have demonstrated the director's leadership, and that the organization's leadership was aware of the areas of improvement and had a clear plan for addressing them; knowing your team and their strengths and areas of improvement is an important and fundamental expectation from every organizational leader.

So why didn't they share their insights on the day? The cognitive culture and the director of the organization were inviting participants to provide critical and constructive feedback, but the emotional culture of the organization did not offer participants the emotional and psychological safety to express their views. This discrepancy denied the director and the leadership team as well as the organization and its members a valuable opportunity for improvement.

While cognitive culture defines expected behaviours and declared values, emotional culture reflects *what people actually do* and the values they hold. When we ignore the emotional culture, we're ignoring what makes people and organizations tick. The ability to tap into the wisdom of their own emotions and to develop and maintain an effective emotional culture is what separates inspirational leaders from leaders who hold and exercise power mainly due to their title and through organizational hierarchies.

Fear and anxiety

Fears and anxieties as described in the example above can undermine leadership. They are further aggravated and heightened by the risks and emotional labour that are embedded in health and social care practice and leadership. Fear of something going wrong, fear of not getting it right, fear of not making the right decision, fear of not being good enough, fear of failure and more. This, combined with the lack of headspace for reflection and the urgency of work and its 'addictive' nature, can lead us to a place where we fear fear itself.

'Mirror, mirror on the wall, who is the fairest of them all?' asked the wicked queen. We have all heard the story. However, reflecting on that story, it can be said that the queen never 'really' asked the question and that she was never interested in its real answer; she only wanted to hear that she was the fairest regardless of whether that was true or not.

In the same manner, the conference participants in the example above seemed to think that in spite of the director's invitation of critical comments, she only wanted to hear applause and see positive comments. This is reflected in the director's statement: 'I was worried about how we're doing but am glad that went well.'

In this sense, the participants considered the director's question as rhetorical and the director as inauthentic, so they mirrored the director by responding in an inauthentic manner.

The director's fear of not being 'good enough' to face the reality of the service is mirrored by conference participants' fear of not being 'good enough' to express the difficulties in the service. This exemplifies the lack of good enough leadership, and such lack of good enough leadership is often projected onto others, resulting in a culture of fear, shame and blame. The leader who pushes the responsibility for poor service, poor practice or poor performance onto others is fearful of facing their own stake and their own role and contribution to that outcome. While this may be conscious or unconscious, and explicit or implicit, doing so creates a culture of uncritical deference, which leads to a fear of raising concerns.

Hence, it's essential for leaders to use every challenge, situation or organizational dynamic as a mirror – to ask themselves 'What is my stake in this?' and encourage others to do the same.

Emotions, fear, vulnerability and authenticity

We attract people who are like ourselves and hence, when we operate from fear, we attract others who also operate from a fear-based place.

This leads to a toxic culture of fear (both conscious and unconscious) and hampers creativity, openness, vulnerability, empathy and authenticity; this is particularly problematic in times that require leaders to create psychological safety.

Instead of suppressing their emotions, employees today expect a workplace that feels less like a workplace and more like a community where they can bring their whole self with all their thoughts, emotions, passion, creativity, vulnerabilities, challenges and enthusiasm.

Employees seek meaningful work that makes a difference, with which they can identify and through which they can find self-expression and achieve that most elusive of Maslow's hierarchy of needs: self-actualization.

Therefore, leadership today can mean serving as a mentor, a cheerleader, an advocate and protector, a resource and a coach.

Coaches don't play ball, but they do mentor, offer guidance and enable authentic human connection and the psychological safety for people to talk about their emotions and feelings and share the burden of their fears and vulnerabilities. This is at the heart of empowering relationships that are foundational for relational leadership. Offering people the opportunity to share their emotions and the time and space for reflection enables people and organizations to wrap emotions in thoughts and develop wisdom and grow.

Freud's (1905) account of a three-year-old boy afraid of the dark is particularly apt. The boy calls out to his aunt from a darkened room, 'Auntie, speak to me! I'm afraid because it's so dark.' His aunt answers him, 'What good would that do? You can't see me.' 'That doesn't matter,' replies the child, 'if anyone speaks, it gets light.'

For practice wisdom to flourish, people must feel that they can share their experience and wisdom as well as their fears and vulnerabilities.

REFLECTIONS

1. If you were to name five emotions that define you and your leadership style, what would they be? In your view, which five emotions would your team or employees associate with you and your leadership style?
2. What is the emotional culture in your workplace, and what are its implications? Is this recognized and explicitly addressed?
3. What is needed to create a more open and validating emotional culture within your organization, and how do you see yourself, your role and responsibility in contributing to, developing and sustaining such an emotional culture?

References

Barrett, K. C. and Nelson-Goens, G. C. (1997) 'Emotion Communication and the Development of the Social Emotions.' In K. C. Barrett (ed.) *The Communication of Emotion: Current Research from Diverse Perspectives* (pp.69–88). San Francisco, CA: Jossey-Bass.

Freud, S. (1905) 'Three Essays on the Theory of Sexuality.' *S. E., 7*, 125–172.

Goleman, D. (1995) *Emotional Intelligence: Why It Can Matter More Than IQ.* New York: Bantam Books.

Marx, K. (1978) 'Economic and Philosophic Manuscripts of 1844.' In R. C. Tucker (ed.) *The Marx-Engels Reader* (pp.66–126). London: Norton & Company.

Morris, M. W. and Keltner, D. (2000) 'How emotions work: An analysis of the social functions of emotional expression in negotiations.' *Research in Organizational Behavior 22*, 1–50.

Siegal, D. (1999) *The Developing Mind: How Relationships and the Brain Interact to Shape Who We Are.* London: Guilford Press.

Weber, M. (1978) *Economy and Society.* London: University of California Press. (Original: *Wirtschaft und Gesellschaft*, 1922.)

• Chapter 8 •

LATERAL LEADERSHIP

Authority and Influence Beyond the Hierarchy

Petros Oratis

> Dr Petros Oratis is an organizational consultant and Co-Founder of The Lateral Space. He is Visiting Faculty Member of the systems-psychodynamic executive postgraduate course 'Inside Dynamics in Organizations' at Utrecht University and has held membership and staff roles at various Group Relations Conferences.

Introduction

Some of the most difficult moments in my career have been when I had to stand out from my peers and lead an initiative. The voice in my mind would typically ask 'Who am I to take the lead?' and 'How will they perceive me?'

After coaching numerous leaders and senior teams, I now know I am not alone in this. This self-doubt is eased when we are formally authorized. But as we grow in leadership, role boundaries become far less settled through hierarchy, and we are expected to negotiate them ourselves. Here lies the paradox that many senior leaders experience: despite developing more confidence in their expertise and ability to lead, they feel socially more insecure about doing so. This is because they are required to *lead laterally*.

This chapter explores the emotional and relational challenges of leading laterally. It deep-dives into the dynamics this entails as well as the psychological models leaders unconsciously deploy. And it offers some principles that can help us in lateral leadership.

If hierarchy doesn't authorize us, who does?

'Everyone on the team will be equal. No hierarchy, no cliques and no titles. If two people think differently, then it shouldn't matter who has the highest rank. Best idea wins, no matter what.'

These were the principles required by Andreas Ehn, Spotify's chief technology officer, when the co-founders hired him to build its tech department, as seen on *The Playlist*, a Netflix dramatized series narrating the beginnings of the music streaming giant (Levin, 2022).

What is described here is a leadership model in which leaders don't rely on their formal authority to reach decisions but instead lead one another laterally based on facts, content and desired outcomes. This lateral leadership paradigm isn't just relevant to start-ups or tech company companies but is also a reality for leaders even within the most traditional hierarchical structures. It doesn't reflect simply an ideology or a trend in leadership values but a necessity due to how work gets organized, the complexity of organizational structures and the nature of challenges that require collaboration across boundaries and levels.

Simply put, if top-down and bottom-up dimensions of leadership are vertical, as it's shaped by hierarchy, lateral is the horizontal dimension of leadership where we have to collaborate with others without a hierarchical relationship or authority over them.

Later in the series, Andreas's principle is put to the test when his peer, Petra Hansson, chief legal officer, convinces the co-founders to close a commercial deal with the record labels in order to secure the company's existence. Andreas considers this move a betrayal of Spotify's purpose and values, while Petra argues that this is the very way to reach them and avoid the company's extinction.

How feasible is the best-idea-wins principle? And if such alignment is so complex, what does it take to lead beyond formal authority?

How do leaders experience lateral collaboration?

As organizational paradigms are transforming into more interdependent working structures, leaders with formal authority are expected to inspire and be at the service of collaboration as opposed to solely command and control the work.

Organizations in the public sector also apply agile principles and create flatter structures, not necessarily to keep up with competition as in the private sector but as a response to their complex environments and to meet the demands of their users. A hospital may introduce horizontal multi-disciplinary teams of healthcare providers to enable targeted holistic care to patients. Universities build research ecosystems that span across academia and industry. In such paradigms, leaders are expected to navigate and enable decision-making on crucial topics laterally.

So, how does it feel to be in these situations and what challenges might a leader experience?

> It's Monday morning and Tara, managing director of a unit, is preparing for her weekly staff meeting, when suddenly Alex, her counterpart in a sister unit, bursts into her office. He's furious that Tara's team have decided to offer a new service without consulting with his unit first, as users might expect the same service from Alex's unit and this can't be offered.
>
> But for Tara's team, this was a no-brainer, as it reduced the pressure they faced as well as the potential for legal liabilities. For Tara, this made Alex's concern seem trivial. Alex's reaction made Tara feel attacked. What hurt her the most was the feeling that Alex was implicitly questioning her integrity and motives.

Is this a conflict about egos, about being excluded from decision-making, about whose power gets displaced? Or is it truly about the factual implications of how one decision is aligned across other parts of the organization? In lateral collaboration, it's often hard to disentangle content from relational issues.

Most leaders dread the prospect that interactions like this may occur. They risk damaging existing collegial relations and how one's integrity is perceived, with the potential implications for reputation that this can imply. On the other hand, the cost of automatically aligning decisions might be too high, as this may result in loss of autonomy and the slowing down or disadvantaging of one's own team priorities and conditions. But what if our peer leaders are holding different operating principles and objectives in mind?

Typically, we might turn to someone higher in rank to make a final decision, but now we have to do it ourselves. The prospect of a friendly supportive colleague turning into a fierce negotiating opponent makes the lateral dimension of work unsafe and can leave leaders feeling like they can't be vulnerable and authentic. This can lead to the work environment being experienced as harsh and lonely. One senior executive told me she found herself spending most of her day aligning with other leaders, without the possibility of authentic interactions: 'I have to use every skill I've got in the book. Like I feel sometimes I'm trying to be the negotiator. Sometimes I'm trying to be the influencer. Sometimes I'm being just an outright dictator.'

It is no surprise that, in most cases, leaders are reluctant to enter lateral interactions where their role accountability isn't clear. In lateral collaboration, the potential for conflict feels far more dangerous than in vertical relations. Imagine a dispute about your accountability with your boss. While you might get frustrated with your supervisor's lack of support or be fearful of their punitive judgement, at least the nature of this relationship is explicit; the differences are visible, and despite potentially difficult emotions, this is psychologically familiar territory. But in lateral conflicts, intentions and boundaries are disputable and can generate higher levels of self-doubt.

As differences are hidden, we might not know what our 'opponent' is capable of. Most importantly in hierarchical relations, there's a clear relational interdependency between a supervisor and a subordinate. But in lateral collaboration, we may not be conscious of our interdependencies until we hit a dead end. In those moments, we might feel like we don't matter to the other leader, who is just fighting for their objective, and if we don't fight for our own, nobody else will. Leaders often describe these situations as 'do or die' or a 'fight to survive'.

The dynamics of lateral collaboration

With such urges to fight, we might expect that lateral conflict is frequent. But emotional outbursts or explicit conflicts, like the one between Tara and Alex, are actually rare. Judgements and aggression typically get swept under the carpet and expressed indirectly. The reason for this avoidance goes beyond displaying a politically correct image. Conflict outside the formal hierarchical structure is simply very threatening.

To understand this, let's consider what happens amongst young siblings during the absence of their parents. When left to their own devices, young siblings tend to self-regulate aggression to achieve some relational cohesion. Or to put it in more simple terms, they tone down their behaviour to avoid killing each other. It's usually when under the parental gaze that all the sibling rivalry drama comes out. So if in lateral collaboration aggression is suppressed, what are the dynamics that self-regulate the relation?

Authority negotiation and covert power assertion

Imagine entering a negotiation. You want to defend your department's interests. If you can't rely on formal rules, you need to find other ways to influence the other parties. There will be a limitation to what you can push forward without hierarchical backup. So you need to display other forms of power. The risk is that you may come across as authoritarian or threatening, so this has to be done in a non-confrontational way. This is what can create the feeling of insincerity and suspicion. Effectively, we are telling our peers, 'I really don't want to, but as a last resort, I will be forced to assert my power, so please take me into account.'

> Ibrahim, director of operations, receives an unplanned request to support a new quality improvement campaign from Yvonne, the service manager.
>
> Ibrahim can only support this campaign if it doesn't put the operations across the entire organization at risk, but Yvonne doesn't see this as an issue. Ibrahim can't simply assert his hierarchical level difference to reject Yvonne's request; this would mean he'd be seen as an authoritarian leader. Instead of protecting his team from the workload, this might result in him damaging them by presenting them as non-cooperative bureaucrats.
>
> So Ibrahim has to set his boundaries in an implicit yet effective way: 'Listen, it's not that I don't want to support your campaign, but without good planning, we don't have the capacity to handle it. Even if you escalate this, the situation won't change. Let's sit down together and see what timing and support could be possible based on our capacity and your needs.'
>
> Ibrahim approaches Yvonne as an equal party, and offers a win-win prospect that can be reached through mutual compromise, but he also implicitly makes her aware of how he can assert his authority if needed.

As hierarchical escalation and formal authority is used less, leadership becomes highly relational. Leaders now reach agreements through relational dynamics. And their ability to lead is not grounded in formal authority but backed by the relations and reputation they build across the organization.

Absolute equalitarianism and obsessive equality

The above power dynamics are present when resolving a dispute and reconciling differences. But such interactions make us aware of our power and seniority differences. While we might accept formal hierarchical differences, and operate explicitly based upon them, we're uncomfortable when exposing differences of power or authority in lateral relations. We want to avoid any feelings of injustice or envy. So an opposite phenomenon, the masking and even denial of differences, characterizes lateral dynamics. This is especially so when we're not forced to resolve differences.

We already noticed in the example of Ibrahim and Yvonne that there's no mention of their level differences, even in relation to whose priority is more important. Leaders and groups who collaborate laterally will strive for absolute equality, at least on the surface.

Often, this comes across as the much-desired working culture of equalitarianism based on the 'best-idea-wins' concept: everyone has an equal voice, everyone's contributions are welcome. But this can work against the quality of collaboration and the decisions it produces. A collaborating group can become obsessed with dividing time and resources between all members equally even though this isn't required. It can become unsafe to consider how an initiative may apply to some but not all parties involved. Discussion may take longer, as everyone must be included because any suspicion as to why they were excluded might attack the group's existence. Decisions are made through consensus. The group strives to sustain cohesion through harmony, oftentimes at the expense of output. In such equality, we may find it harder to suggest we're impacted or disadvantaged by certain decisions. We may forget that our opinion may not be helpful in certain discussions and so on.

The shifts between the dynamics of equality, negotiation and conflict may even occur within the same relation, which explains why some leaders find the different lateral roles they're forced to take on exhausting. We can imagine what political and relational skills we need to develop in order to navigate. But how have we instinctively learnt these skills?

Early life models

> Raul, course leader of a bachelor's degree course, gathered all peer course leaders to co-create university policy on the use of artificial intelligence

(AI) tools in students' assignments. He was taken aback when Shiva, peer course leader, dismissed his initiative, implying he was simply struggling to accept that openly accessible AI is here to stay and eventually all students will use it.

Some course leaders agreed, others remained indifferent. Raul felt completely misunderstood. He took pride in embracing new developments but wanted to proactively organize for them too. The response of the peer leaders dismissing him left him feeling unfairly unsupported and convinced that he now had to stubbornly create and apply his own workaround.

As a child, Raul had experienced his parents being unreasonably strict, and if there was no way to convince them to show leniency, he would find his own way to do his thing. In contrast, he could be quite cheeky with his brothers, often bargaining with them to get his way. In his interaction with his peers, his unconscious emotional experience resembled more of his early parent–child dynamic instead of his sibling dynamic. Why was that?

The complexity of the relational experience in lateral collaboration is that the one who now holds power over our autonomy may not be an authority figure but a peer. Usually, in our earliest experiences where we've felt frustratingly dependent on another's power, it's been with figures of vertical authority like parents or teachers. And the way we've learnt to negotiate outside formal authority has been with siblings and peers in the playground. Lateral dynamics can activate instinctively familiar emotions of all vertical and lateral early-life relational models. What emotionally blocks us most is when current dynamics feel too similar to painful experiences of being dismissed, excluded, misjudged or disempowered that didn't have a happy ending.

When I ask leaders to reflect on how their leadership style has been formed throughout their careers, it's striking to see the links between early career authority figures and later interactions with peer leaders. Leaders often describe times in their early careers when they've been subjected to what they perceive as authoritarian leadership that's caused them intense performance anxiety or a loss of freedom to act. But as they've progressed to hold senior leadership roles, it's rarely direct hierarchical bosses who've activated similar anxieties; it's peers. The descriptors used for an authoritarian boss early in a career are the same as those used for peer leaders who challenge authority or autonomy now.

This explains how primitive anxieties can be activated in lateral interactions. It also helps us understand why our first impression of a challenging peer leader is likely to be that of an authoritarian. It's not that all senior leaders consistently display such behaviours and motives. But the intensity of lateral dynamics can by default create an emotional response of survival in which even the most benign peer leaders may come across as fiercely egocentric when negotiating boundaries with us.

How can we navigate lateral collaboration?

Such understanding helps us make sense of lateral dynamics differently. Organizations all have a significant degree of vagueness that leaders have to resolve laterally, and the dynamics of this task are emotionally, relationally and politically demanding. If we accept these as inherent to this form of collaboration, we might be more resilient to the emergence of difficult emotional memories from the past.

When collaborating laterally, it helps to be as explicit as possible. The tendency to avoid conflict, hide differences and appear collaborative can create suspicion and misinterpretation. Instead, it can benefit collaborative leaders to take a step back and jointly frame the collaborative task, the individual risks and conflicts raised, the differing levels of investment, the most helpful roles for collaboration and the decision-making criteria that might best be applied.

The more leaders speak of their concerns and personal challenges, the more trusting an environment can become. And since lateral dynamics are in the core power dynamics, it's more effective to explore differences from a place of vulnerability than through the assertion of power.

Towards the acceptance of interdependency

Accepting vulnerability and dependency on others is perhaps the most challenging factor of lateral relations at work, especially for senior, well-established leaders. We start life completely vulnerable and totally dependent on our caregivers. Our development path aims to use our own powers to become self-reliant. But as we mature in our career, we may develop the illusion that losing our autonomy equals becoming impotent, and accepting our vulnerability equals losing our leadership gravity.

In organizations, markets and societies today, laterality has become the norm. This gives the illusion and expectation that vertical authority and hierarchy are obsolete. But the promise of equalitarianism isn't entirely honest. Organizations, societies and nations are still run by formal authority. We may only be thinking of authority as a privilege gained to exercise accountability, which often comes with significant statutory and legal liability. Paradoxically, formal accountability remains the same, yet we're required to fulfil it by leading laterally.

Reflecting on my own struggles in taking up lateral leadership, I've learnt that my early life experiences with siblings and classmates have created internal emotional responses in me that are not always helpful or real. Instead of struggling internally or avoiding lateral leadership, the key to negotiating lateral leadership boundaries is to invest relationally in lateral connection with others. Such an approach allows us to transcend the pull of early emotional responses and stay focused on what the task demands.

REFLECTIONS

1. What situations in your leadership role force you to collaborate laterally, and what emotions do you then experience?
2. What routines would you typically deploy when you'd rather protect yourself from intense lateral dynamics? How do you think your behaviour impacts collaboration?
3. What were your early-life relational roles (with parents, teachers, siblings, classmates) that defined how you navigate power differences today? How might you experiment differently in your lateral leadership today?

Reference

Levin, B. (Executive Producer) (2022) *The Playlist* [TV series]. Netflix. https://www.netflix.com

• Chapter 9 •

SIBLING LEADERSHIP

Stepping Away from the Role of Overbearing Parent

Val Parker

> Val Parker is a psychodynamic psychotherapist, group analyst, supervisor, teacher and writer. She currently runs a private practice from her home in Oxfordshire. She is a clinical supervisor on the Qualifying Course at the Institute of Group Analysis, London, a training group analyst for the Qualifying Course in Group Analysis in Tirana, Albania, and a visiting lecturer on the University of Oxford Psychodynamic Studies programme, the Oxford Foundation Course in Group Analysis and the Diploma in Groupwork Practice at Turvey. Her book *A Group-Analytic Exploration of the Sibling Matrix: How Siblings Shape Our Lives* was published by Routledge in 2020.

In our world today, with rare exceptions, we have become accustomed to a form of leadership in which we promote our leaders into isolated parental positions, expecting them to make decisions for us and clear up the mess when things go wrong. But those whom we nominate as leaders are in fact our *peers*, and expecting them to behave as though they are above us will inevitably set up power dynamics which can stifle collaboration and diminish our creativity and independence.

In this chapter, I argue that if our leaders are encouraged to work alongside their teams as nominated and responsible *siblings* rather than overbearing parents, they will be better equipped to foster cooperative and respectful teamwork and deal more effectively and creatively with rivalry and competition.

I have always struggled to understand why football managers are instantly sacked when their team loses a few matches or why chief executives are blamed and dumped by disgruntled shareholders when profits slump, replaced by someone who is given the impossible task of 'turning things around' and delivering instant dramatic results. Is this really the answer?

I think we invest far too much in our leaders – too much remuneration, too much responsibility and too much expectation. This is detrimental to the teams they head, continually under pressure to adapt and reorganize themselves, and it encourages a culture of passivity and blame which not only stunts creativity and confidence but can also result in a worrying trend of infantilization, ruthlessness and dehumanization.

After the killing of George Floyd in 2020, the leadership consultant Gianpiero Petriglieri gave a chilling indictment of the dangers of charismatic leadership:

> Before we offer the usual mix of heartfelt sentiments and practical solutions...those who are leading businesses or...educating future leaders, must also admit a hard and shameful truth. The dehumanisation we condemn is not just on us – it is in us, and a large part of business leadership itself...a view of leadership that, put bluntly, is a means to get your way, and get stuff done – in style. If you can do that, you are a leader. If you can't, you are not. This is the hollow core of popular portraits of leadership as an individual virtue or as a set of tools that let a person bend others' minds and move their bodies too. (Petriglieri, 2020)

Yet, we as a human species are natural collaborators. Our ancestral forebears, *Homo Sapiens*, were hunter-gatherers who survived because of their unique ability to share and collaborate (Boehm, 1999, 2012; Harari, 2011). We are team-builders, whose need for one another is rooted in our DNA. But we have become overwhelmed by greed and competition, endlessly fighting over land and possessions, obsessed with 'having all we can get' at the expense of not only our fellow humans but of the entire planet.

To build a more collaborative world, we must urgently rethink what we are demanding from our leaders. We need to stop expecting them to be like parents who have all the answers and foster leaders who can be alongside us and inspire us – leaders who do not have to shine or dominate or make decisions for us but who will listen and understand. I believe that if we turn to our sibling selves, we may find some answers.

The sibling matrix

Within us all is a relational area emanating from our sibling experience, initially developed in our upbringing with our brothers and sisters and continued throughout our lives in our interactions with those alongside us. I have called this our 'sibling matrix' (Parker, 2020).

Our siblings have a seminal influence on our social development, but this is frequently overlooked (Brown, 1998; Brunori, 1998; Shapiro and Ginzberg, 2001). Yet it is with our siblings that we first discover that we are not alone. It is with our brothers and sisters where we learn to share, to collaborate, to have respect for others, to recognize our differences, to fall out and make up, and where we learn to cope with rivalry, competition and envy.

Sibling relationships are often complex and difficult, but they are also rich and full of potential. Siblings can cause one another immense pain and distress. But they can also be an invaluable source of inspiration and support and are often the best teachers, as illustrated in the following vignette.

Nathan

One of my patients had for many weeks been distraught about his young son Nathan's difficulties with eating. We talked about it endlessly, devising strategies, trying to understand the child's communications, wondering about food intolerances. Then one week he came and told me that there had been a surprising breakthrough.

Nathan's older brother Matt had intervened. Gently and quietly, Matt had coaxed Nathan to eat, talking about his own dislikes and difficulties and how sometimes he got stuck with things too. It did not take much but Nathan had felt heard and understood by a peer, and it was transformative. Nathan was never going to respond to his parents' anxiety and frustration. He needed someone who could sit alongside him and offer encouragement. Only his older brother could do this.

This was leadership at its best – supportive, collaborative, respectful and enabling – vital human qualities which belong with our siblings. So how can we use these experiences, developed throughout our lives, to inform us as leaders?

The 'sibling' orchestral conductor

Before I trained as a psychotherapist, I was a musician. From my vantage point in orchestras, I experienced leadership from many different conductors. They fell into two distinct categories: those who believed that the orchestra was their instrument and those who saw themselves as *members* of the orchestra. These two positions created very distinct types of performance and induced very differing experiences for the players.

Conductors in the first category see themselves as the sole creator of the musical interpretation. Their performances can be thrilling – tight, disciplined, powerful, exciting, energetic. They rely on players who look up to them and who will play *for* them, seeing the orchestra as their servant. Often narcissistic, they will evoke this in the players. Orchestral members may feel inspired, but they will be keen to please and look for praise and attention, which is likely to lead to heightened competition and rivalry amongst them.

Conductors in the second category view themselves as group members tasked with a specific responsibility – to hold things together and provide a framework for an unfolding, *collaborative* effort. Players will be encouraged to express themselves, to listen and respond to one another and to contribute to an unfolding joint interpretation. The players will feel more involved and more mutually supportive of both one another and the conductor. They will feel more like siblings.

To achieve success as a conductor *within* an orchestra means metaphorically stepping off the podium and getting among the players, having the humility to recognize that everyone has a vital contribution to make. The conductor will be more like a facilitator or enabler – a fellow sibling taking charge of an unfolding mutual process. At its best, this will bring deep satisfaction to both the players and the audience, who will also be partaking in an intimate experience rather than observing a performance which is there to impress. An orchestra led in this way will feel more like a family in which everyone's contribution is valued, and there is likely to be much less rivalry and competition among the players.

Being *alongside* our team members rather than above them is a crucial way to build trust and cooperation. This can indeed be challenging in a large organization such as the NHS, where necessary structural procedures tend to encourage hierarchical leadership. In the example below, the paediatrician Collette demonstrates how she has managed to achieve collaborative working in a very busy department.

Teamwork in a paediatrics department

Collette is the clinical lead for paediatric mental health in an overstretched department in a busy city hospital. This complex role entails working with many different departments: eating disorders, child and adolescent mental health services, intensive care and A&E. Collette believes that to manage and coordinate such a range of disciplines, it is essential to work from within the team:

> We are quite fragmented – all the disciplines work differently. I see my job not as telling my colleagues what we need or what to do but as listening and trying to get an overview. I can only do this if I work inside the teams – doing the work they do so that I can understand their perspectives and ways of working. I need to understand how it works for *them*. If I stand back, I feel that I am missing something. Everyone needs to lead. I have to pull it all together.

This way of working is counter to her training, where she was encouraged to stand outside her team and focus on managing procedures – nominating tasks and assigning roles.

Collette thinks her innate inclination to lead from within comes from her early upbringing in India. Right from the start of her life her preoccupations were with her *peers* – her sister, cousins and friends who all grew up together. Her parents didn't feature in her mind. They would provide discipline but were not involved in her emotional life. When she and her sister were sent to boarding school in the UK, they relied on one another for survival.

Later as a doctor in Africa working in very culturally diverse teams, the sense of non-hierarchical teamwork felt familiar – it was 'a given' that everyone would muck in and pull their weight.

Her current team is ethnically diverse with a strong female component. She notices how more traditionally trained (often white male) consultants try to impose leadership by taking over – questioning treatment plans or talking to families without consulting them – and how confusing and undermining this is for her colleagues.

Sibling-led leadership may well be difficult for others to understand – it can appear as if no one is in charge. Managers and bosses who need to see results or who have strong egos will disrupt the collaborative work, undermining the achievements and not appreciating the teamwork. But sibling leadership at its best allows everyone to thrive and feel that their contribution is valued.

Facing sibling rivalry and competition

Sibling issues can provoke powerful emotions. These can give us vital clues not only as to what might be happening for us as individuals but also to what is occurring in the organization. The more we understand the origins of our responses, the more empowered we are to act differently – to be more open and inclusive, to understand the judgements and assumptions we make and to react less impulsively and more compassionately when we meet challenges.

In the following example Eli, who had recently been given a leadership promotion, found herself unable to manage her new team. It was only when she understood the systemic sibling rivalries infiltrating her organization, and recognized their striking similarities with her own family, that she could fully embrace her new role.

Sibling rivalry in an organization
When the founders decided to retire, they assumed that the institution they had regarded as 'family' would continue to function in a collaborative way. But their lack of sufficient preparation for this big transition meant that sibling rivalries held at bay by their firm grip on the organization immediately began to flood the system.

The three incumbents, sadly ill-prepared for taking over, could not agree on anything. Unable to manage their differences, they decided the only solution was to split the organization into three sections, which they would each head.

When the new director took over control of Eli's division, he immediately began to impose his authority by undertaking a total restructuring. Eli's boss Jen was promoted onto the executive board, and Eli was invited to step into her position as head of department. She was aware that taking on this role would probably cause some resentment among her colleagues, but she was not prepared for what ensued.

Things changed immediately. She found herself alienated and isolated, and her team impossible to manage. Formerly amenable colleagues became uncooperative and complaining. She felt increasingly out of control – the more assertive she became, the more her team resisted. Her confidence collapsed. In complete despair and on the point of handing in her resignation, she decided to come to me for help.

As she told me about her situation, we recognized that not only was she caught up in toxic organizational dynamics but also that the situation had an uncanny resonance with her own family matrix. She was the second eldest of six children. Her parents were unable to cope and left Eli and her sister to run the household. Eli's sister was bossy and demanding, constantly putting her down, just like Jen.

She had coped by turning her attention to their four younger siblings, sorting out their quarrels, dressing them, taking them to school.

Here at work, Eli found herself once again abandoned by the 'parents', caught between a bossy older sister and a bunch of unruly youngsters. Seeing these resemblances allowed Eli to take stock. She began to see that everyone was struggling with dynamics which were deeply entrenched in the system. The more she tried to 'fix' things, the worse things became. Her team members needed to know that they were in it together and that she would listen and support them while they accustomed themselves to the new situation.

We can see that the chaos being handed down the ranks of this organization resulted from leaders who had made no provision for their succession. As in families, destructive sibling issues are bound to arise when succession is not handled with real thought and preparation, as Wilke highlights:

> When changes are imposed on work teams, sibling preoccupations surface to prevent the working through of the breakdown of relations between the institutional parents and their dependents. Team siblings adopt envy-preventing strategies, engaging in collective self-idealisation by forming sisterhoods or brotherhoods against the organisational parents to protect themselves from disillusionment and individualisation. ...the new leaders often act like stepparents and make their teams feel like fostered siblings. (Wilke, 2014, p.xix)

In this atmosphere, it was almost impossible for the new generation to take over. Eli's director had tried to impose his will on the division rather than letting his colleagues help him settle. The only way to shift the chaotic dynamics effectively was to adopt a more collaborative style of leadership, but this was going to take time to achieve.

Elevated siblings

One of the difficulties for Eli was the speed of her promotion. Those in leadership positions, however they handle their authority, will inevitably be envied and resented. Many competent staff members are given leadership positions as part of a natural career progression, and it can be tempting to try to hold authority by stepping into a parental position. But as Obholzer and Miller suggest, leaders who act in this way will be seen as bossy siblings who are above themselves, only adding to the resentment:

> Leaders and managers are experienced as siblings who have reached 'above their station' and, in the cauldron of unconscious institutional processes, are thus perceived as 'fair game' for a process of bringing them down to earth. It would be wrong to see such activity only in terms of an envious attack on a sibling rival; it would be equally inappropriate to sweep these processes under the carpet to pretend that they don't exist. (Obholzer and Miller, 2004, p.41)

However, trying to avoid envy by undermining one's power and success can be equally unhelpful. Doing oneself down to avoid envy belongs very firmly in the sibling matrix – a trait Kreeger describes as 'envy pre-emption':

> [a] term that categorizes certain defences, strategies or manoeuvres aimed at negating or reducing envious attack. It includes devaluing of the self, appeasement and placatory activities, such as self-damage. (Kreeger, 1992, p.393)

In families, siblings are constantly jostling for positions and care about how they are seen by one another, as do team members. If we are to lead from a horizontal position, then we need to know our sibling selves intimately and be constantly aware of how we are responding to all challenges including competition and comparison.

Conclusion

Sibling leadership is not easy. It requires being able to negotiate the fine balance between putting oneself amongst others and being able to stand back and view the situation as a whole. It also involves tolerating inevitable rivalries and finding a way to foster mutual respect. But sibling leadership has enormous potential to inspire others and enable everyone to thrive.

I would like to end with some words from Petriglieri:

> Ask people what makes a great leader in theory, and they will often point a lofty vision. But ask them about a leader that they trusted and felt good following in reality, and they will point to something else. A sense of being reassured, a strong connection that made them feel safe. (Petriglieri, n.d.)

This is exactly what sibling leaders can offer.

REFLECTIONS

1. How do you think your own sibling matrix impacts on you as a leader?
2. Think about what position you tend to take in groups. How might this link to your sibling experience?
3. What changes might you wish to make to your teams to encourage a sense of collaboration and siblinghood?

References

Boehm, C. (1999) *Hierarchy in the Forest: The Evolution of Egalitarian Behaviour.* Cambridge, MA: Harvard University Press.
Boehm, C. (2012) *Moral Origins.* New York: Basic Books.
Brown, D. (1998) 'Fair shares and mutual concern: The role of sibling relationships.' *Group Analysis 31*, 315–326.
Brunori, L. (1998) 'Siblings.' *Group Analysis 31*, 307–314.
Harari, Y. (2011) *Sapiens: A Brief History of Humankind.* London: Vintage, Penguin.
Kreeger, L. (1992) 'Envy re-emption in small and large groups.' *Group Analysis 25*, 391–412.
Obholzer, A. and Miller, S. (2004) 'Leadership, Followership, and Facilitating the Creative Workplace.' In C. Huffington, W. Halton, D. Armstrong and J. Pooley (eds) *Working Below the Surface* (pp.33–48). London: Karnac Books.
Parker, V. (2020) *A Group-Analytic Exploration of the Sibling Matrix: How Siblings Shape our Lives.* New York and London: Routledge.
Petriglieri, G. (n.d.) The Good Enough Leader. http://gpetriglieri.com/in-a-crisis-holding-matters-more-than-vision

Petriglieri, G. (2020) To Fight Systemic Racism, Protest 'Leadership' – Not Just Leaders. *Fast Company Magazine.* www.fastcompany.com/90513406/to-fight-systemic-racism-protest-leadership-not-just-leaders

Shapiro, E. L. and Ginzberg, R. (2001) 'The persistently neglected sibling relationship and its applicability to group therapy.' *International Journal of Group Psychotherapy 51*, 3, 327–341.

Wilke, G. (2014) *The Art of Group Analysis in Organisations: The Use of Intuitive and Experiential Knowledge.* London: Karnac Books.

• Chapter 10 •

THE DISAPPOINTED AND THE DISAPPOINTING

Learning for and about Leadership

Christopher Scanlon and John Adlam

> Christopher Scanlon is an independent psychosocial researcher, consultant psychotherapist, Founder Member of the Association for Psychosocial Studies (APS) and Principal Fellow of the Higher Education Academy.

> John Adlam is a consultant psychotherapist and independent researcher, Founder Member of the APS and of the Henderson Heritage Group, and former Vice-President of the International Association for Forensic Psychotherapy.

No man is an island, entire of itself; every man is a piece of the continent, a part of the main.

JOHN DONNE, 1624

Disappointment, when it involves neither shame nor loss, is as good as success; for it supplies as many images to the mind, and as many topics to the tongue.

SAMUEL JOHNSON, 1836

Introduction

To be disappointed is to be human; it is also human to be disappointing.

Experiences of disappointment are an inevitable aspect of human life in groups, organizations and communities. In this chapter, we identify disappointment as a central experience in all 'psychosocial practice' and we consider how it might be taken seriously, reflected upon together – and perhaps even creatively mobilized as an aspect of leadership. By 'psychosocial practice', we refer to all work that sits at the intersection of what is psychological, pertaining to the human mind, and what is sociological, pertaining to the way in which society is ordered (or disordered!). More specifically, in speaking of (psycho-)social work or practice, we have in mind all those relational and structural dynamics that pertain to life in groups and communities and have to do with welfare, health, social care and the criminal justice system.

Moments of disappointed-ness and disappointing-ness – whether anticipated, experienced in the here and now or remembered – pervade all aspects of this work and play out not only in the interface between the socially excluded and 'the Authorities' but also the interface between frontline psychosocial practitioners and those charged with leading and managing these organizations.

And yet systems of care seem generally to operate as though disappointment is not an unavoidable outcome but rather an impossible one. Disappointment, if it is considered at all, seems to be disconnected from or pushed resolutely aside (perhaps after a brief but perhaps secretly luxurious wallow); it is not to be sat with, processed, puzzled through or, as we shall go on to propose, practised.

'Pathways', 'progression', 'recovery', 'solutions', 'striving', 'succeeding', 'surpassing', 'onwards and upwards'... we who have leadership roles within these complex and often chaotic systems can run you off a catchphrase or a position statement in no time at all, so long as the direction of travel is positive and unilinear.

But disappointment? We haven't had that spirit here in a long while now. True, there's a complaints procedure and a feedback system, but the messaging is clear: these roads all lead to the Rome of customer/consumer satisfaction – rather than taking more seriously their dissatisfaction.

As for the idea that 'we', the builders and denizens of these shiny new offices, outpatient clinics or visitor centres, might be even the tiniest bit disappointed in 'you', the service users who pass through our sliding glass doors, we are professionally and personally insulted at such a suggestion!

But consider this: the harder the disappointed/disappointing reality of *global* climate disaster and the war(s) that accompany it presses upon us, the less likely it is in these postmodern times of ours that the organizational corporate literature of the more *local* 'Authorities' will acknowledge even the possibility that such-and-such a service might be a disappointing place from which to seek help, or within which to work. If services fail to factor in disappointment, this is a denial or disavowal of the inevitability that we are going to disappoint and be disappointed.

A key function of management or leadership roles in human services is, therefore, to create and participate in spaces and places where we all can engage more deeply and more deliberatively. In more open, and therefore perhaps riskier and messier, reflective conversations about what it might mean to be both disappointed and disappointing.

Learning from the 'Diogenes Paradigm'

Consider the adventures of the migrant, homeless, dissident street philosopher Diogenes, who at one time dwelt in a barrel in the ancient 'agora' or gathering space in Corinth. The relationship between the figures of Diogenes and his contemporary and counterpart, Alexander the Great, King of Macedonia, the renowned military commander and conqueror, can be used to illuminate the psychosocial dynamics of the systems of care (see Scanlon and Adlam, 2022).

This chapter is founded in our practice and long experience, separately and jointly, as psychosocial practitioners, supervisors, managers, consultants and researchers. However, rather than bring vignettes, 'real' or composite, to illustrate our line of argument, we have deployed episodes from our own retelling of the stories of Diogenes and Alexander, inviting you to hear these tales as parables that illuminate present-day dynamics and dilemmas.

1. Practising disappointment?

Our first story concerns Diogenes and his own way of managing the psycho-societal dynamics of his time:

> The Athenian townspeople came upon Diogenes kneeling with his begging bowl at the feet of a stone statue, his dogs beside him. When they asked him why he was engaged in this apparently futile pursuit, he replied that he was practising disappointment.

By publicly and satirically practising disappointment in this way, Diogenes invites his audience to notice that if one is homeless, displaced or destitute, one might as well beg from a lump of stone as expect to be seen, heard, recognized or offered hospitality and proper psychosocial accommodation. His is the wary and world-weary wisdom of lived experience: he has read both the claim form and the complaints policy, and he's not buying either of them.

'Better get used to it,' we might imagine the statue saying, and we partly hear Diogenes passing on this wisdom to those in search of asylum, housing, welfare benefits, a place in a care home or treatment for cancer today. On a deeper level, Diogenes is practising disappointment so that he may get the better of it; or, more subtly, get better at it. He wants to sharpen the edge of his disappointment, bring it to life and make it work for him rather than find himself tangled up in (self-)defeat.

In our story, Diogenes is not in despair – either about himself or about the world around him. He is 'simply' declining to expect an appointment. We say 'simply' because it's not easy being him, and a lot of emotional work and discipline goes into taking up this position.

Anyone responsible for offering appointments to the excluded would do well to remember that the 'won't-be-appointed' may for very good reasons hold no truck with the would-be-appointer.

2. When Diogenes met Alexander

Alexander the Great, whom we briefly mentioned earlier, perhaps needs less introduction than Diogenes (the metropolitan elite are always more visible and celebrity-studded than the 'little people'). Alexander was probably the most powerful man in the world at the time.

The figure of Alexander in our retelling of these stories stands as an embodiment of the power of the system of care, and all those who hold leadership roles and power within it.

Our second story concerns Alexander's encounter with the contrasting figure of Diogenes, who here stands for the apparently powerless outsider:

> The leaders of all the Greek City States had appointed Alexander to lead the war against Persia.
>
> He decided to host a celebration and asked the townspeople of Corinth which local dignitaries should attend. They suggested (perhaps with a subtle shade of satire of their own) that he invite Diogenes who, of course, declined to keep the appointment.
>
> Alexander then assembled an outreach team and went to accost Diogenes in his barrel. Impressed with Diogenes, whom he found 'intelligent and articulate', and sorry to see him in apparently reduced circumstances, he asked if there was anything he could do for him. Diogenes said that Alexander was blocking out the sun and told him to get out of his light.

Notice here that it's Alexander who must taste the fruit of disappointment. Alexander has never been thwarted in any desire, and like our contemporary masters, he denies the very possibility of disappointment. It's not going to happen to him and he knows that no one dare find him disappointing, and so he is very much taken by surprise when Diogenes doesn't 'turn up' for his appointment.

Diogenes, in contrast, expects disappointment; he makes it into a central part of his domestic-and-foreign policy and therefore cannot be waylaid by it. More than this, he declines to identify as disappointed because he declines to recognize Alexander's authority to book him an appointment in the first place.

The other theme to pick out is the idea of truth-telling – specifically the practice of speaking truth to power. Alexander is more used to settling arguments with his sword and so it's very dangerous to refuse any offer he might make; he is the naked emperor who is unused to being told the truth. Yet in the face of Diogenes' truth-telling ('you're blocking the sun'), Alexander (at least momentarily) renounces his violence: he steps aside but stays in the conversation. Diogenes is not subjected to performance management or disciplinary measures, nor required under the Vagrancy Act to pack up his barrel and be on his way. The conversation is valued in and of itself. For Alexander to be disappointed in this way and yet to stay in the conversation is truly a moment of great leadership.

3. Of knots, and have-nots: Alexander at Gordium

We, the authors, do not idolize either of our protagonists, and the figure of Alexander in his imperialist violence can be seen as far more antisocial than Diogenes: might is right, right is mighty and enough said. Our third vignette is one in which he does not set aside his sword:

> The 'Gordian knot' was famous for its seemingly unfathomable intricacy, and legend had it that anyone who untied it would become King of all Asia. Alexander, who coveted that title, gathered the great and the good at Gordium to witness him making the attempt. Discovering that the knot was indeed too complex to be unravelled, he cut through the knot with his sword so as not to lose face. Because he was Alexander and his sword was still sharp, nobody disputed his claim to the Kingship.

We suggest that there are no health and social care challenges that are not bound up, like a colossal psychosocial or socio-economic Gordian knot, with the offering or withholding of care, treatment or more ordinary human concern. Alexander at Gordium denies this complexity and therefore denies, godlike, that there is any sort of limit to his power or the reach of his authority. He abolishes disappointment with one slash of his blade. The challenge for (psycho-)social work leadership is to stay with the complexity (see Moore, Chapter 3 of this book), to be wary of the temptation to 'slash the knot' by offering simplistic 'solutions' to complex problems.

To work in our systems of care is to risk being faced with the inevitable disappointment that comes with the acknowledgement of our own and others' frailties and mortality. More importantly, it also represents a moral injury (consider here the position of Alexander's audience at Gordium) caused by having to witness, or participate in, high-stake work situations that demand that, as practitioners and leaders, we must do-what-has-to-be-done in ways that offend our sense of what is considered right or wrong in more ordinary human relating.

Ring-fencing the 'agora'

Bonnie Honig (1996) suggests that much (perhaps even all?) psychosocial work takes place in these morally injurious situations that she describes as 'dilemmatic spaces'. These are spaces that open when conversations must take place about things that do not fit together, or that contain inherent contradictions, and when actions are demanded that will inevitably disappoint.

In our terms, these spaces may be likened to the 'agora' – the marketplaces and other protected public spaces in which, standing in the shoes of Alexander, latter-day 'Authorities' encounter the figure of Diogenes in all his latter-day guises and in which there is a possibility that truth-telling might take place. Contemporary trends tend towards the closing down of such spaces as being counter-countercultural and seditious, whereas our invitation to the (psycho-)social work leadership is to follow Alexander's example from our second story by keeping the agora open: welcoming the conversation and dealing honestly with the disappointment that will then come to light.

Within such dilemmatic spaces, there will always be those who are more obviously disappointed and those who are more obviously disappointing. Sometimes the distribution of disappointment is between service users and practitioners working in the system of care (Diogenes begging from a statue, for example); at other times, between these same practitioners and 'the management' (depending, for example, where each grouping stands in relation to any given 'knotty' problem).

To be effective in such work requires practitioners to work in multi-disciplinary and inter-agency teams within which the felt sense of disappointment is not evenly distributed and is constantly shifting around. One day, it is with the disappointed/disappointing manager; the next day, the social worker; and the day after, the community nurse. Each of these have different experiences of professional power and positioning. Rather than be quietly grateful that today it is somebody else's turn to be disappointed, the pressing question is how to work with team/group dynamics together.

Disappointment is a personal experience, but it is also a systemic issue in which there are no observers or bystanders – only participants. However, as practitioners struggling with our own relative disappointment, we must always remember the different ways in which we are identified with the power of the figure of Alexander in our story. In contrast, service users and their communities (including those of our fellow human beings who are excluded from services) hold the Diogenes position: they have far less power and are rarely well positioned, although they may value the ground that they do stand on.

In terms of management and leadership of these conversations, we want to suggest that 'managing the business' (including the delivery of formal care plans, treatment regimes, contracting meetings, etc.) and learning how to learn from each other and work together, though systemically related, are distinct activities that utilize distinct ways of knowing that need to be developed through different types of conversation in different spaces and places.

We suggest that our three stories of different kinds of encounter and performance in the agora can shine a light upon the leadership challenges in (psycho-)social work from a new and perhaps unexpected angle. We hope it's clear from our first story that the old guy and his dogs won't be content until they come across a leader who will admit the realities of disappointment!

Second, we hope we have shown that there is some kind of particular quality to 'agora-like' spaces that needs to be protected and ring-fenced so that truth-telling can happen inside organizations, be heard and not be quashed by disciplinary power.

Third, we make our own plea for celebrating complexity (and cultural diversity, for that matter) rather than taking one's sword to its intricate knots and reducing it, as Alexander did at Gordium, to shreds of simplistic slogans. In a world in which would-be citizens are made homeless in far greater numbers and far more rapidly than the existing homeless population could ever be 'resettled', 'zero tolerance' pronouncements of this kind must always come with zero tolerance of disappointment built into them. Alexander kept face at Gordium – but he lost Asia.

Leaders of many different ilks tend to undermine agora-like spaces (such as Reflective Practice Groups, or temporary learning communities such as awaydays), either directly, by disdaining to attend themselves, or indirectly, by pulling away those who would attend to other 'more pressing' tasks. This is not to say that 'other things' are sometimes not just as important.

Rather, we invite leaders to consider that when they absent themselves from these more collective space conversations, or require others to be elsewhere, it is the very idea of the importance of staff-group meeting spaces that is being devalued and dis-appointed (for further discussion of the place of Reflective Practice Groups, see Scanlon, 2017, 2019; Adlam, 2019). There might from this perspective be nothing more central and essential to a healthy and well-functioning authority and hence a better functioning team than the upholding of the boundary stones of the agora.

If we can create and maintain reflective spaces where truths can be told, we may be better able to (re-)connect with our shared humanity – to feel, think and behave as if an injury to one is an injury to all – to (re-)position ourselves, to borrow Donne's immortal phrase, as pieces of the continent, as parts of the main.

Not to do so, we argue, is to risk becoming and remaining stuck, aggrieved, resentful, monadic – island fortresses in (imagined) total control of our perimeters as the waters rise and the darkness falls about us.

REFLECTIONS

1. What are some of the obstacles to learning from experience that you have encountered that might have had to do with your own or others' disavowal of feelings of disappointment?
2. The figures of Diogenes and Alexander in these stories both take up antisocial or anti-societal positions in relationship to the complexities and disappointments of group and social and civic life. Who do you most closely identify with – and why?
3. Can you identify any 'agora-like' protected spaces for truth-telling, between the included and the excluded, in any of the places you have worked in? If so, what sustained them, and what pressures did they come under? If not – any ideas why not?

References

Adlam, J. (2019) "Scallywag battalions": Reflective practice groups with multidisciplinary teams in mental health and social care systems.' *Organisational and Social Dynamics 19*, 2, 168–185.

Donne, J. (1624) *Devotions Upon Emergent Occasions and Death's Duel*. Reprinted 1999. New York: Vintage.

Honig, B. (1996) 'Difference, Dilemmas and the Politics of Home.' In S. Benhabib (ed.) *Democracy and Difference: Contesting the Boundaries of the Political* (pp.257–278). Princeton, NJ: Princeton University Press.

Johnson, S. (1836) *The Lives of the Poets: A Selection* (2009, p.422). Oxford: Oxford University Press.

Scanlon, C. (2017) 'Working with Dilemmas and Dis-appointment in Difficult Places: Towards a Psycho-Social Model for Team-Focussed Reflective Practice.' In A. Vaspe (ed.) *Psychoanalysis, the NHS and Mental Health Today: Understanding the Needs of Patients and Staff* (pp.115–134). London: Karnac.

Scanlon, C. (2019) '"Practising Disappointment": From Reflective-Practice-in-the-Organisation to Deliberative-Practice-in-the-Community.' In C. Thornton (ed.) *The Art and Science of Reflective Practice in the Organisation* (pp.76–84). London: Routledge.

Scanlon, C. and Adlam, J. (2022) *Psycho-social Explorations of Trauma, Exclusion and Violence: Un-housed Minds and Inhospitable Environments*. London: Routledge.

• Chapter 11 •

RELATIONAL LEADERSHIP IN A CRISIS

Jim McManus

> Jim McManus is National Director of Health and Wellbeing for Public Health Wales. He was previously President of the Association of Directors of Public Health and Director of Public Health for Hertfordshire County Council. He has extensive experience of crisis and disaster leadership and recovery. He is a chartered psychologist.

Sooner or later, most leaders will find themselves navigating through some kind of crisis. For the purposes of this chapter, I define crisis as an event, situation or phenomenon that destabilizes the team, organization or system in which we operate, which goes significantly beyond the parameters we would normally expect to find ourselves in.

Throughout my career as a director of public health, I've led organizations and communities through several crises, including: HIV (the human immunodeficiency virus), which attacks the body's immune system; SARS (severe acute respiratory syndrome); the H1N1 swine flu pandemic in 2009; and a range of other natural and man-made incidents. However, the SARS-CoV-2 pandemic (Covid-19) was by far the most protracted and multi-faceted in its impact. Jean-Claude Larchet describes the pandemic as having:

> ...surprised, disoriented and disorganized, in all their structures, all the countries of the world... It has profoundly affected lifestyles and mentalities for a long period. It called into question the forms of organization of modern States, showed the fragility and flaws of a globalized system that we believed to be stable... The science we thought was sure turned out to be full

of hesitations and uncertainties. The biological and genetic techniques that we believed to be all-powerful have proven to be groping. (Larchet, 2021, p.7)

Reflecting upon my experience, I've come to understand that the single most important lesson of leading in a crisis is that relationships are foundational to successful crisis management. Having a crisis plan and models for crisis leadership will help, but relationships and keeping oneself and others safe and effective will make or break the results of your efforts (McManus, 2020). Models can neither substitute nor compensate for a leader's understanding of the complexity of issues in a crisis and their ability to engage in it dynamically.

Planning for a crisis: necessary but not sufficient

Good literature will help you plan, but of course, on its own, this isn't enough. There are multiple definitions of crisis leadership, and familiarity with at least one of these is valuable. Coombs and Holladay (2010) have made classic and substantial contributions in this field, but much of it has been focused on public relations and communications.

There are also multiple models for crisis management which can be used in preparation and planning for crises, from Marker's freely available online guide 'Essential Guide to Crisis Management I Smartsheet' (Marker, 2020) to legislation such as the Civil Contingencies Act (2004) in the UK, which specifies how statutory agencies and other actors such as infrastructure and utility providers should plan for, mitigate and respond to crises (United Kingdom Parliament, 2004).

But none of these models prepare leaders for how to lead relationally during a crisis, especially during a crisis which is protracted and dynamic such as the SARS-CoV-2 pandemic.

Given the experience and impact of the pandemic, most research and reflections have gone beyond communication and public relations and taken better account of the dynamic and relational nature of crisis leadership. For example, Kim (2021) suggests core attributes of crisis leadership such as 'clear, fast, frank communication; a high degree of collaboration; sharing of information; decision-making and fair prioritization; building trust; and competency'. While Wu *et al.* (2021) emphasize a multi-faceted leadership approach and highlight the crucial importance of knowing how to build and keep relationships.

How a leader behaves is every bit as important as what a leader decides during a crisis. Tapping into the opportunities to harness the skills and insight of others is directly proportional to how willing the leader is to adopt an approach which balances discernment, listening, collaborating and decision-making. This stands in contrast to the assumptions we often have about 'heroic' leadership. The character of the leader needs to be far more about relator-discerner (one who relates effectively with the context and colleagues and is able to comprehend what may seem obscure) and adaptor than hero in a crisis. Indeed, what matters most is the persistent practice of virtues like relating, discernment, commitment to solidarity and exercise of good judgement underpinned by good relational sense (Poole, 2017, pp.48–55).

Using the principles of authenticity, integrity, honesty and fairness and embracing the ethics of public service, I adopted four principles to act as way-markers for my leadership approach during the Covid-19 crisis, and for the remainder of this chapter, I will focus on these four way-markers.

1. Way-marker: Relationships are foundational to keeping your bearings

Much of the literature remains descriptive of what attributes and behaviours are effective at navigating crises rather than how they are applied or synthesized for action in real time. All of the attributes or styles summarized above are adaptive.

But a good crisis leader needs a 'compass' or some way-markers to help sense when and how to adapt, dynamically, sense change and adjust plans and tactics accordingly.

In my experience, there are five golden rules in crisis leadership. These are the ability to:

1. sense change

2. adjust dynamically

3. plan for a crisis

4. expect your plan to inevitably be disrupted the minute you enter the crisis by something you didn't consider or plan for (an unexpected consequence or systemic factor which was largely unpredictable)

5. understand and maintain relationships, which is perhaps your most crucial resource. Relationships are the currency of crisis leadership. Relations with others can help you sense capabilities, frustrations, innovation and exhaustion or confusion among the people you seek to lead.

A model I find helpful in leadership is the four leadership domains shared with me while undertaking leadership studies at Ashridge Hult Business School as a Health Foundation Generation Q Fellow (Wiggins, Smallwood and Marshall, 2017).

There are four domains across which a leader needs to understand their motivations, impact and actions (see Figure 11.1). Personal self-understanding as well as interpersonal skills and style are as important as having technical knowledge (e.g., epidemiology), as is the contextual knowledge of the organization and situation one works in.

In my experience, this remains a go-to tool to reflect on how I lead in crises. At one stage during the Covid-19 pandemic, I kept this model in my journal and reflected weekly, and sometimes daily, on how I was leading and what I'd learnt. My other way-markers all build on this model as tools which can be used in and across these four domains. Together, these form one of the most important things a leader can do in a crisis, which is to discern, repeatedly, what we should do (Joubert, 2019).

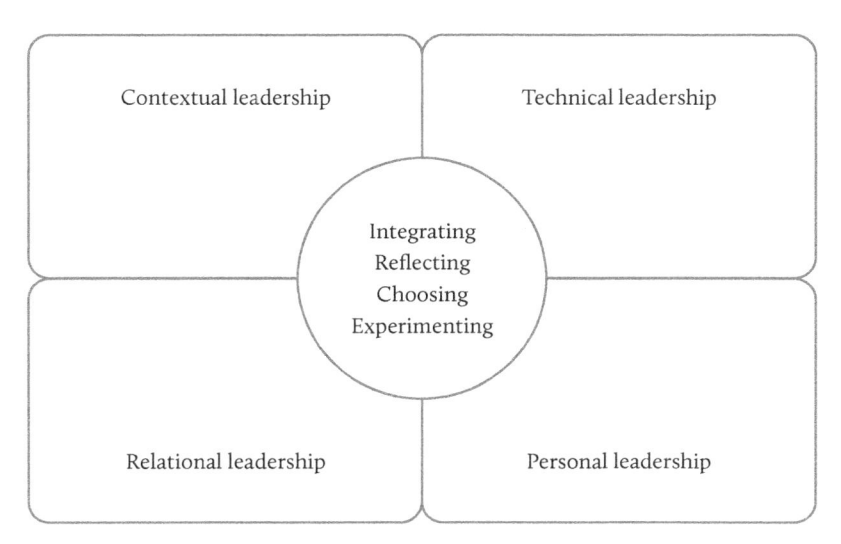

FIGURE 11.1: FOUR DOMAINS OF LEADERSHIP

Source: Wiggins and Smallwood, 2018, https://www.bluemorph.co.uk/docs/journal-of-management-development-article-2018.pdf. Reproduced with permission.

2. Way-marker: Say hello to prudence – good judgement while the world is churning

Prudence is often wrongly understood as caution – timidity, taking the least serious course. Dismiss this idea. Prudence is the practical virtue of discerning the right course of action, and in a crisis, prudence is a continuous exercise in leading and discerning, which you must hone and harness.

Leadership studies are rediscovering the importance of character strengths and the practice of virtues like justice for leaders (Wang and Hackett, 2020). Qualities like integrity, humility and empathy are increasingly being recognized as central to a relational concept of leadership. Within this, the application of prudence is being recovered and re-emphasized (Wilson and Newstead, 2022).

The classic setting out of prudence in Roman Catholic thought, deriving from St Thomas Aquinas, sees prudence as having three parts: considering the various means to achieve an end, deciding which is best, and choosing to do it (Labourdette, 2016, pp.7–48). Applying prudence in considering as many outcomes as possible and their effects on people and aims is a crucial task for discernment, and in a crisis, it is a virtue which needs to be honed and applied regularly (Pine, 2022, pp.13–65). Prudential judgement is helped by regularly checking and reappraising what you know about the situation and doing this with others. In my experience, prudence is a better predictor of outcome than raw instinct and far less dangerous in application.

We have a model of a visionary leader who comes to the fore during crises, charting a course through uncertainty. But where do they get the course from? If they're not exercising those three parts of prudential wisdom, how on earth do we know this is not a reckless course? Yes, effective leaders need to craft a compelling direction, but it needs to resonate with the evidence and with stakeholders and pivot as circumstances change.

Prudence is also important to help retain your moral compass as a leader. Major crises often present leaders with morally complex choices that can impact lives, economies and societies. Ethical leadership becomes paramount as leaders grapple with the trade-offs between short-term survival and long-term wellbeing. The practice of prudential judgement and engaging others is important here. Using prudence to weigh the consequences of decisions, and relationships to ensure you are acting transparently, and being accountable for the outcomes is vital. It requires a strong moral compass to navigate the grey areas inherent in crisis management.

The prudent leader working through the four domains is a better guide to action than the lonely hero working on instinct and vision alone. A prudent leader will: deconstruct and analyse – even if quickly; be clear on what the challenges and options are; understand their components and what can be done about each of them; and triangulate this with what they know from their relationships. Prudence can also help you understand when to collaborate, when to direct and when to coach. Crises almost always come with moral complexity; let prudence guide you.

3. Way-marker: 'Ressourcement': harness what you and others know – some of it will help

While crises bring new and uncharted territory, there is almost always something in the tools and technologies you and other stakeholders have acquired or been trained in you can use. Somebody somewhere will have knowledge of value in discerning the right thing to do.

I have sometimes had people say to me that listening to or engaging too many people is a sign of weakness. I couldn't disagree more. It is a sign of seeking as much information and as many perspectives as possible to be able to exercise prudential judgement on an issue. Discerning what weight to put on perspectives and advice is a challenge, and being clear on what principles and approaches you are taking is important.

This is where 'ressourcement' – going back to the sources of what you and others know – comes in. Triangulating these sources is part of good prudential judgement. It should be obvious that you can't rely solely on yourself for this.

Do not be afraid to go back to first principles and foundations of knowledge, both for you and others. As a public health professional, I was trained to structure my approach to an issue, including understanding what evidence there was, and get my questions right before deciding on acting. Getting people who know their fields and their disciplines, and returning to the sources of your practice, almost always brings tools and lessons, even if only for one part of the problem. A good media colleague and a good epidemiologist in a public health crisis are both equally valid. Get them to trust their training, and you should too. This requires humility, but it is also dependent on relationships. If you take the lonely hero mode of leadership, you deprive yourself of knowledge and skills you do not have.

4. Way-marker: Self-care

A final way-marker is that of caring for yourself. You are no use to others if you can't find some way of caring for yourself. This is perhaps the area most leaders did poorly on during the early stages of the pandemic. Many leaders during the pandemic experienced a sense of failure that they could not do more. Many experienced trauma. To compound this, a number of us, myself included, experienced threats and intimidation from people who were opposed to one or other course we may have advocated, such as those vehemently opposed to vaccinating people or those who felt that Covid-19 did not exist.

The weight of leading in a crisis can, if you choose to take it all on yourself, be crushing. As can the weight of being seen to pretend everything is fine. An honest leader who admits their struggles in the right place, but keeps their eye on the hoped-for destination, and who is seen to care is a powerful motivator for others. It can also provide permission for people to be honest about their doubts, fears and struggles.

The lonely hero model at best is risky. At worst, it can destroy you and others if you go to a place of not caring for yourself or others and react to advice as if it were criticism, which entrenches a sense that you are right despite others having different views or experience. Self-care is vital, because without it you become turned inward upon yourself in a crisis, and that is the last thing you should do. Being realistic about challenges and realistic about impact is vital. Having produced guides to trauma and self-care for various audiences from public health teams and pastors, experience tells me self-care creates better leaders (McManus, 2022).

Conclusion: authentic crisis leadership is relational and provisional

While crises are inherently disruptive and damaging, they can ironically also offer unparalleled opportunities for growth and transformation. In this vein, sometimes the best way to learn to lead in a crisis is by leading through one or being able to be mentored by someone who has. Leaders who navigate crises successfully can emerge paradoxically both wounded and with new skills, a refined leadership style and a deepened ability to work with others.

But we need to reflect on lessons learnt during the crisis – not just our success but also where we have hurt others and been hurt. I am convinced that one of the enduring mistakes from the Covid-19 pandemic will be rushing to return to business as 'pre-Covid usual' without letting people take stock, learn and identify where to go.

Crisis leadership should seek the good of everyone in and through a crisis. This requires a dynamic interplay, a dance of discernment if you will, between and across various issues and stakeholders, always founded in relationships and dependent on good practical wisdom and judgement. Leaders need to balance the need for action with the importance of involving stakeholders in decision-making. This in turn requires a delicate equilibrium between centralizing power for rapid response and empowering individuals to contribute their expertise. Successful crisis leaders are emotionally intelligent and authentic.

All of this is a way of saying that to be an authentic leader in a crisis is to be a relational one. Valuing people, valuing the ends, discerning the right course and caring for yourself and others are all vital. Your leadership needs to take all of this into account. We will have more crises in our world as climate change, emerging disease and food insecurity continue. All of these challenges require good crisis leaders, who are relationally wise and not heroically stand-alone.

REFLECTIONS

1. What steps would you take in a crisis to understand yourself, others and the context of what's occurring?
2. People know things that can help; how will you ensure that you listen to a range of voices?
3. Authentic leadership matters; how do you ensure you remain authentic during a crisis?
4. How do you care for yourself and others during a crisis?

References

Coombs, W. T. and Holladay, S. (eds) (2010) *The Handbook of Crisis Communication*. Malden, MA: Wiley-Blackwell.

Joubert, S. (2019) 'A Well-Played Life: Discernment as the Constitutive Building Block of Selfless Leadership.' In J. Kok and S. C. dan den Heuvel (eds) *Leading in a VUCA*

World: Integrating Leadership, Discernment and Spirituality (pp.139–150). Cham: Springer Open.

Kim, S.-J. (2021) 'Crisis leadership: An evolutionary concept analysis.' *Applied Nursing Research 60*, 151454.

Labourdette, M. (2016) *La Prudence: Grand Cours de Théologie Morale II*. Les Plans-sur-Bex and Paris: Parole et Silence.

Larchet, J.-C. (2021) *Petite théologie pour les temps de pandémie*. Paris: Éditions des Syrtes.

Marker, A. (2020) Essential Guide to Crisis Management I Smartsheet. www.smartsheet.com/content/crisis-management-guide

McManus, J. (2020) Keeping Yourself and Others Safe: Leadership in the Age of COVID-19. Centre for Mental Health. www.centreformentalhealth.org.uk/keeping-yourself-and-others-safe-leadership-age-covid-19

McManus, J. (2022) *Resilience, Trauma and Pastoral Recovery* (p.34). London: Faith Action and Guild of Health. https://gohealth.org.uk/blog/resilience-trauma-and-pastoral-recovery-a-briefing-for-faith-communities

Pine, G. (2022) *Prudence: Choose Confidently, Live Boldly*. Huntington, IN: OSV.

Poole, E. (2017) *Leadersmithing: Revealing the Trade Secrets of Leadership*. London, Oxford, New York: Bloomsbury Business.

United Kingdom Parliament (2004) Civil Contingencies Act 2004 c.36. Statute Law Database. www.legislation.gov.uk/ukpga/2004/36/contents

Wang, G. and Hackett, R. D. (2020) 'Virtuous Leadership.' In D. C. Poff and A. C. Michalos (eds) *Encyclopedia of Business and Professional Ethics* (pp.1–5). Cham: Springer International Publishing.

Wiggins, L. and Smallwood, J. (2018) 'An OD Approach to leadership development: questions and consequences.' *Journal of Management Development*. Emerald Publications. https://www.bluemorph.co.uk/docs/journal-of-management-development-article-2018.pdf

Wilson, S. and Newstead, T. (2022) 'The virtues of effective crisis leadership: What managers can learn from how women heads of state led in the first wave of COVID-19.' *Organizational Dynamics 51*, 2, 100910.

Wu, Y. L. *et al.* (2021) 'Crisis leadership: A review and future research agenda.' *The Leadership Quarterly 32*, 6, 101518.

• Chapter 12 •

HOW TO BUILD CO-PRODUCTION: INVOLVING PEOPLE AS REAL PARTNERS

Don't Wait to Put Your Ducks in a Row

Clenton Farquharson

> Dr Clenton Farquharson CBE is a disabled man with extensive experience in health and social care. He holds numerous influential national roles including Chair of the Think Local Act Personal partnership board and Trustee of the Social Care Institute for Excellence. Clenton is also a part of the NHS Assembly, Quality Matters, the Race Equality Foundation and Skills for Care. He holds an honorary doctorate from the University of Birmingham, is a trainer, consultant and coach and was named in Disability News Services' list of influential disabled people.

Introduction

My journey in understanding disability and its influence on my leadership approach is deeply intertwined with my identity as a proud Brummie and the son of Windrush parents from Jamaica who faced their own challenges in adapting to life in the UK.

This heritage has instilled in me fortitude and a unique perspective, shaping my approach to leadership, care and support.

My secondary school years in Birmingham, facing the silent battle of undiagnosed dyslexia, marked the beginning of my unconscious encounter with the complexities of disability.

Developing coping strategies without recognition or support for my dyslexia, I navigated an educational system that was unaware of my needs. This phase of my life underscored the critical need for understanding and support in education systems, a principle that resonates with the communal values I inherited from my Jamaican heritage.

At 27, I found myself in a situation where my intervention was crucial. Witnessing a young woman in danger, I acted instinctively to prevent her from being assaulted, a decision that led to me being stabbed 26 times.

This harrowing experience, while highlighting the darker aspects of human nature, also illuminated the strength and fortitude inherent within me – qualities I attribute to my Jamaican heritage and the legacy of my Windrush parents.

The aftermath of this incident was profound.

It left me as a wheelchair user, transitioning me from an invisible disability of dyslexia to a visible physical disability.

This shift brought new challenges and insights, emphasizing the diverse needs within the disability community.

It was a stark reminder of the vulnerabilities we all can face and the extraordinary circumstances that can thrust us into the realm of disability.

This incident, coupled with the experiences of my youth, profoundly shaped my views on vulnerability, bravery and trust.

Living with disabilities, both invisible and visible, taught me the strength in vulnerability and the necessity of nurturing trust in both personal and professional spheres.

The philosophy of Ubuntu, emphasizing humanity's interconnectedness, along with the communal values instilled by my Jamaican roots, have greatly influenced my leadership approach: I am because we are.

These experiences guided me to prioritize community, connection and mutual support in my professional endeavours, recognizing the strength that comes from our shared humanity and collective experiences.

As a leader, my journey underscores the value of lived experience and the importance of embracing vulnerability and trust.

It highlights the need for a communal approach in care and support, aligning with the principles of co-production, respect and inclusivity.

Building co-production at the senior level requires us to incorporate the wisdom and insights of those who draw on care and support services.

Valuing our experiences, as I have learnt through my own, can revolutionize these services.

This journey, marked by personal trials and the rising strong spirit inherited from my parents, is a testament to the evolving power of personal experiences in shaping understanding and effective leadership. This work, indeed, has changed me, illustrating the profound impact of courage, fortitude and community in overcoming life's most daunting challenges.

To create meaningful change in social care services, we must embrace co-production – a collaborative approach that involves people who draw on care and support as genuine partners.

Waiting for the system to change itself is not effective, and we must take action now to build co-production at the senior level.

In this chapter, we explore how to reimagine care and support by involving people as real partners, treating them with compassion and incorporating their wisdom into every level of care and support service.

It's time to stop waiting for our ducks to magically align and start taking proactive steps towards co-production.

Partnering with people who draw on care support

Waiting for all the ducks to be in a row before partnering with people who draw on care support is a mistake.

Authentic engagement requires involving people as real partners, both at the point of care and support, and in the organizations where care and support system decisions are being made.

This means recognizing and valuing people's experiences and perspectives and actively seeking their input in decision-making processes.

It's crucial to move beyond the traditional organizational boardroom table and ensure diverse representation of people who draw on care and support in all levels of decision-making.

Treating people as fellow human beings, not boxes to be ticked

This is about extending empathy and respect towards others, recognizing our humanity and individuality rather than reducing us to mere categories or tick boxes.

It involves treating people with dignity, considering their unique experiences, perspectives and needs, and engaging with us on a personal level rather than making assumptions or generalizations based on superficial characteristics.

Treating people as fellow human beings, not boxes to be ticked, means valuing diversity and inclusion, and embracing the richness that comes from different backgrounds, cultures and identities.

It involves actively listening to others, seeking to understand their thoughts and feelings without judgement and fostering meaningful connections based on mutual respect and understanding.

It requires acknowledging the complexity and diversity of human experiences and recognizing that people are more than just labels or categories.

It means refraining from making snap judgements or assumptions based on stereotypes, biases or preconceived notions, and instead taking the time to engage with others in a genuine and respectful manner.

Treating people as fellow human beings, not boxes to be ticked, is an essential aspect of building inclusive and equitable communities where everyone feels valued, heard and respected.

It promotes empathy, compassion and understanding towards others and helps create a world where individuals are seen and appreciated for their unique identities and humanity rather than being reduced to tick boxes on a list.

Genuine partnership in co-production means treating people who draw on care and support as fellow human beings, not just as boxes to be ticked off on a to-do list.

This requires acknowledging and valuing their stories, experiences and perspectives.

People have valuable wisdom and insights to share, and it's important to create spaces for us to be heard and incorporated into care and support services.

Compassion should be at the heart of care and support, and we need to reintroduce art, stories and humour to bring back the human touch in an increasingly science-based world.

Reimagining care and support

To build co-production at the senior level, we need to reimagine care and support services.

This means tearing down the old ways of doing things and building something new.

We need to challenge the status quo, question existing norms and be open to new ideas and perspectives.

Wisdom gained from the experiences of people who draw on care and support should be acknowledged, listened to and incorporated into every level of care and support service.

This revolution in care and support can only happen when we actively involve people as partners and embrace co-production as a guiding principle.

Co-production is not about waiting for our ducks to be in a row but about taking proactive steps towards meaningful collaboration with people who draw on care and support.

Building co-production at the senior level requires reimagining care and support services, treating people with compassion and valuing our wisdom and insights.

It's time to think beyond the traditional organizational boardroom table and actively involve people as real partners in decision-making processes.

Only then can we create a revolution in care and support that truly serves the needs of those who rely on these services.

Let's not wait any longer but take action now to build co-production at the senior level.

Positive change requires intentional effort

Positive change in any context, whether it's in our personal lives, organizations or society at large, requires intentional effort and a deep understanding of key principles.

I offer four essential concepts that are foundational to creating positive outcomes: lifting others up, examining values, co-production and recognizing 'the water we swim in'.

These concepts highlight the importance of genuine trust, respect, dignity and equalizing power dynamics in our pursuit of change for the better.

1. Lifting others up

Lifting others up is about recognizing and valuing the inherent worth and potential of every individual.

It means actively supporting and empowering others, whether it's through mentoring, coaching or advocating for their rights.

Lifting others up also involves fostering a culture of inclusivity, diversity and equity, where everyone's voices and perspectives are heard and respected.

When we lift others up, we create a positive ripple effect that contributes to a more compassionate and cohesive community and, ultimately, leads to better outcomes for all.

By lifting others up, we foster collaboration, innovation and collective problem-solving, which can result in positive outcomes such as increased productivity, creativity and satisfaction among individuals and groups.

Lifting others up also helps to build a culture of trust, where individuals feel valued and motivated to contribute their best efforts towards achieving shared goals.

Additionally, lifting others up can lead to improved relationships, reduced conflicts and enhanced wellbeing, creating a positive impact on individuals' lives and the broader community.

2. No change without examining values

Values are like a compass that guides us towards a better direction.

Values are fundamental beliefs and principles that shape our thoughts, actions and decisions.

They serve as a moral compass, providing us with a framework for making choices and navigating through life.

When we fail to examine our values, we risk making decisions that may not align with our true beliefs and principles.

It can lead to inconsistencies in our actions and create internal conflicts.

Without a clear understanding of our values, we may find ourselves making choices based on external influences, societal norms or short-term gains rather than on what truly matters to us.

Examining our values is essential for personal growth and development.

It allows us to become aware of what truly matters to us, what we stand for and what we aspire to be.

It helps us make decisions that are aligned with our authentic selves and empowers us to live a meaningful and fulfilling life.

Values also play a crucial role in driving positive change in society.

Many social movements and reforms are rooted in a collective examination of values, challenging existing norms and advocating for justice, equality and human rights.

By examining our values and being aware of the values of others, we can foster empathy, understanding and respect towards diverse perspectives, leading to positive societal changes.

In essence, the phrase 'No change without examining values' highlights the significance of introspection, self-awareness and reflection on our values as a prerequisite for personal growth, meaningful decision-making and societal progress.

It emphasizes the importance of aligning our actions with our core values to create positive change in ourselves and in the world around us.

Examining values involves critically reflecting on our beliefs, biases and assumptions that influence our actions and decisions.

It requires being open to feedback, being willing to challenge our own perspectives and continuously learning and growing.

Without examining values, change efforts can be superficial or unsustainable, as they may not address the root causes of problems.

When we take a deep dive into our values, we gain clarity on our motivations, align our actions with our principles and create a solid foundation for meaningful change.

Examining values can lead to transformative change by helping us identify and challenge harmful attitudes or practices that may perpetuate inequality, discrimination or injustice.

By aligning our values with our actions, we create congruence between our beliefs and behaviours, leading to increased authenticity and integrity in our relationships and interactions.

Examining values can also foster empathy, compassion and understanding towards diverse perspectives, promoting a more inclusive and equitable environment where everyone feels valued and respected.

3. Co-production and 'the water we swim in'

Co-production is a collaborative approach that involves individuals with lived experiences, professionals and communities working together as equal partners in designing, delivering and evaluating services, policies or initiatives.

It acknowledges that individuals are experts in their own lives and recognizes the value of their unique perspectives and contributions.

'The water we swim in' refers to the societal, cultural and systemic context in which we operate, which shapes our perceptions, beliefs and behaviours.

Co-production and recognizing 'the water we swim in' can lead to more effective and sustainable outcomes by promoting ownership, engagement and shared responsibility among stakeholders.

When individuals with lived experiences are actively involved in decision-making processes, their insights and expertise can lead to solutions that are more relevant, inclusive and impactful.

Co-production can also foster trust, mutual respect and understanding between professionals and communities, leading to stronger partnerships and better outcomes for all involved.

4. Genuine trust, respect, dignity and equalizing power
Genuine trust is a foundational element of co-production.

Fragile trust: handle with care
Trust is like a delicate flower that needs to be nurtured and cared for in order to bloom and flourish.

It takes time to grow and develop, but it can be easily damaged or lost with just one careless act.

Trust is the foundation of healthy relationships, whether it's between friends, family or romantic partners or in professional settings.

It's built on honesty, reliability, consistency and integrity.

Trust allows for vulnerability, open communication and mutual respect.

Just like a flower, trust requires attention, effort and mindfulness to maintain and protect it.

It's a precious gift that once broken can be challenging to fully restore.

So it's important to handle trust with care, cherish it and always strive to be trustworthy in our actions and words.

Trust is built through open communication, transparency and mutual understanding.

It requires acknowledging and valuing diverse perspectives, listening to the voices of marginalized and vulnerable groups, and being responsive to their needs and aspirations.

Trust is also fostered through accountability, integrity and consistency in actions and decisions.

When trust is established, it creates a positive and inclusive environment where people feel safe to share their ideas, concerns and aspirations, and are willing to work together towards common goals.

Respect and dignity: guiding principles
Respect and dignity are like a beacon that guides our interactions and relationships with others.

They are fundamental aspects of human interaction that recognize and value the inherent worth, individuality and rights of every person, regardless of their background, beliefs or differences.

Respect and dignity are like the sun that shines upon us, providing warmth and illumination to our interactions.

They foster a sense of understanding, empathy and compassion, creating an environment where people feel valued, heard and acknowledged.

Respect and dignity are like the foundation of a strong and healthy relationship.

They build trust, promote inclusivity and cultivate mutual understanding.

They create a safe space for open communication, where differences can be discussed and resolved with civility and respect.

Respect and dignity are like a mirror that reflects our own values and character.

They show our true selves, how we treat others and how we wish to be treated.

They remind us to be mindful of our words and actions, and to consider the impact they may have on others.

Respect and dignity are like a precious treasure that should be cherished and upheld in all aspects of life.

They are essential in our interactions with family, friends, colleagues and strangers and even in the digital world.

They promote harmony, cooperation and positive social interactions, contributing to a more inclusive and compassionate society.

In summary, respect and dignity are like guiding principles that shape our interactions with others, foster healthy relationships and promote positive social interactions.

They are invaluable virtues that should be embraced and practised in our daily lives, creating a world where everyone is treated with dignity, respect and fairness.

Respect and dignity are also key principles of co-production
Respect involves recognizing and valuing the unique strengths, abilities and contributions of all stakeholders, regardless of their background or status.

It means treating people with fairness, empathy and compassion, and honouring their rights and autonomy.

Dignity involves recognizing and upholding the inherent worth and humanity of every individual and ensuring that their voices and choices are respected and valued in all aspects of decision-making and service delivery.

When respect and dignity are embedded in co-production efforts, it creates a culture of inclusivity, where everyone's perspectives and contributions are valued and respected, leading to more effective and sustainable outcomes.

Equalizing power distribution

Equalizing power refers to the concept of balancing or levelling the distribution of power or authority among different individuals or groups.

It aims to ensure that power is not concentrated in the hands of a few but rather distributed fairly and equitably to promote equality and prevent abuse or misuse of power.

Equalizing power can be applied in various contexts, such as social, political, economic and interpersonal relationships.

For example, in social justice movements, equalizing power may involve advocating for marginalized groups to have equal access to opportunities, resources and representation.

In politics, it may involve creating checks and balances to prevent one branch of government from having too much power over the others.

In the workplace, it may involve promoting diversity and inclusion to ensure that power and decision-making are not limited to a select few but are inclusive and representative of all employees.

Equalizing power can also involve addressing power imbalances in interpersonal relationships, such as in partnerships or friendships, to ensure that all parties have an equal say and influence in decision-making and that one person does not hold disproportionate power over the other.

Overall, equalizing power is about creating a more equitable and just society where power is distributed in a balanced and fair manner and where all individuals have the opportunity to participate, contribute and thrive.

Equalizing power is a fundamental aspect of co-production

Power imbalances can be inherent in social, economic and political systems and can create barriers to meaningful participation and engagement.

Co-production seeks to challenge and transform these power imbalances by creating opportunities for all stakeholders to have an equal say in decision-making processes.

This may involve redistributing power and resources, amplifying the voices of marginalized groups and ensuring that decision-making structures are inclusive and participatory.

Equalizing power is essential to ensure that co-production efforts are equitable and that the benefits of collaboration are shared by all people and groups of people.

In conclusion, co-production offers a promising approach to problem-solving and decision-making that is rooted in trust, respect, dignity and equalizing power.

By recognizing the water we swim in and the precious gift that is a trusting relationship and by actively working to create an environment that fosters these principles, we can create more inclusive, effective and sustainable outcomes.

REFLECTIONS

1. How do your personal values align with the values of your organization when it comes to inclusivity and respect for diverse perspectives? Can you identify any gaps or areas for improvement in how you or your organization engage with people who draw on care and support services?
2. In your professional interactions, especially with those who draw on care and support, how do you actively build and maintain trust? What steps can you take to ensure that power dynamics are balanced and that all voices are equally heard and valued in decision-making processes?
3. Consider a recent project or decision-making process you were involved in. Were the insights and experiences of people who draw on care and support meaningfully incorporated? What practical steps can you take in future projects to ensure these individuals are treated as genuine partners and not just as boxes to be ticked?

• Chapter 13 •

SUPPORTING PRACTITIONERS WORKING WITH UNCERTAINTY, COMPLEXITY AND RISK

It *is* Rocket Science!

David Shemmings

> David Shemmings OBE PhD is Emeritus Professor of Child Protection Research, University of Kent, and Visiting Professor of Child Protection Research, Royal Holloway, University of London.

In November 2022 at the University of Kent we celebrated the tenth anniversary of the International Centre for Child Protection, established by me and Professor Jane Reeves. I decided to call my short talk marking the event 'Child protection practice: It IS rocket science!'. In about ten minutes (I cut my presentation, to give Professor Eileen Munro longer!), I tried to make the point that, whilst unbelievably complex, much of rocket science, indeed space travel generally, can be reduced to numbers and equations.

Child protection and safeguarding, on the other hand, cannot, and as a consequence, it is much harder to assess, for example, the risk to a child. In 2012 Professor Jane Barlow and colleagues undertook a *Systematic Review of Models of Analysing Significant Harm*. They comment early on in the report that child protection professionals, whilst being good at gathering information, are not always comfortable when analysing it (a finding that emerges in numerous Local Child Safeguarding Practice Reviews – formerly Serious Case Reviews – as well as Ofsted inspections). The authors also refer to a study in 2008 by Shannon Dorsey and colleagues who found that, in effect, child protection assessments were… (wait for it)… 'only slightly better than guessing'. Thus, we begin to see just how hard the assessment of risk actually is in practice. Although these authors came to their conclusions some 15 years ago, with the exception of some recent approaches, each of which relies on direct observations of parent–child interactions rather than self-report measures – and often a lot of training – things are not much different today.

Why is this – why is it so difficult to assess 'risk'? Arguably, it's because when a professional leaves a family after a visit, they do not know what is actually happening 'behind closed doors', and it's also because 'risk' is a socially defined construct. What one person sees as 'risky', another may not, and, to complicate matters further, definitions of 'risk' can change over time as well. I find this regularly when running training sessions.

I show a documentary film clip in which there are a number of potential child welfare concerns. I then ask participants to discuss where their initial thinking is taking them. I always find a range of responses, from 'Remove the child into care, (with a view to returning them if things demonstrably improve in the family) to 'No further action'. This wide chasm is noted whether or not the participants are from the same professional group. Over the past ten years, I have run this exercise with thousands of participants, so, at face value, their reactions feel reasonably authentic and reliable.

There is, however – and thankfully – a simpler and more effective way to reduce the imprecision when trying to understand how parents/carers might be placing their child at risk and, *on paper at least*, it's fairly simple: it's by developing and maintaining as much trust as possible, for family members to feel confident enough to tell the worker what they think the risks are and how they are struggling. But they are only likely to do this if they believe that the worker is genuinely there to help them. Having followed a number of social workers over many months on home visits and meetings, Professor Harry Ferguson and colleagues convincingly paint a detailed picture of what this looks like, when it 'works'. Their 2022 article on 'relationship-based practice' gives many examples of how and when the development of a 'trusting relationship' is able to work for the benefit of all family members but especially children and young people.

The reason for taking quite a while to get the point of the title of this chapter is that leaders can only really lead when they appreciate fully what they are leading. To be effective in the field of child protection, practitioners need to be able to work comfortably with uncertainty and complexity. To be able to assess risk, they need to relate to families so that they trust them, but to do that, managers and leaders need to offer exactly the same experience to practitioners that they, in turn, need to offer family members.

Leaders and practitioners need to be – or become – adept at appreciating and then applying the insights of a number of key writers on the subject of relationship-based practice. I'm thinking here of Harry Ferguson, David Howe, Gillian Ruch, Adrian Ward, Peter Fonagy and Claudia Megele (who summarizes much of this in her 2015 book *Psychosocial and Relationship-Based Practice*). They will also benefit from revisiting some of the early pioneering writers on relationships, such as Wilfred Bion, alongside Donald and Clare Winnicott.

One of Bion's and the Winnicotts' pivotal ideas, discussed by Harry Ferguson and colleagues in their 2022 paper, is that of anxiety 'containment' with family members. But because the 'primary task' of child protection professionals is saturated in anxiety, as a result of the uncertainties when assessing 'risks' and 'strengths', empathizing with others' anxieties is fraught with challenges. Lest the reader jump to the conclusion that this is all about unrealistic, 'soft' interpersonal qualities, years out of date, Professor Donald Forrester stresses the need for workers to be able to use 'good authority', because empathy without direction and purpose is likely to end up misplaced (Forrester *et al.*, 2020). And authors also stress the need to understand the effects of structural inequality and poverty on the relationship, hence they also draw upon the work of Professors Brid Featherstone, Sue White and Andy Bilson.

As the development of sustaining, reliable and predictable relationships between practitioners and families is *a* – if not *the* – key task and, to be achieved and sustained long-term, it needs to be mirrored within organizations between leaders and professionals, then the obvious question is: how can leaders help promote and facilitate its progress? One way to do this is by rethinking what we mean by 'supervision'.

Professor David Wilkins at Cardiff University is fast becoming a 'go-to' person as a result of his research programme on supervision in child welfare and protection services. David and his colleagues at Cardiff have undertaken a series of studies where they have directly observed supervision sessions. They have looked for a number of features in these sessions, including 'support for practice, analysis and critical thinking, emotional support, empathy for the family, child focus, clarity about risk and decision-making' (Wilkins, 2017).

They have found overall, however, that managers and supervisors asked mostly closed questions and offered lots of advice. Interestingly, this is what the early pioneers of 'relationship skills research' – Robert Carkhuff, Bernard Berenson and Charles Truax – also found after observing hundreds of members of the 'helping professions' when working with clients/patients/service users. Unfortunately, David Wilkins and colleagues report that they didn't observe much by way of 'emotional support'.

Although not a social worker myself, I was for a time a deputy area organizer in a local authority, which meant I offered supervision to a range of practitioners. I always tried to separate the 'hour' into about 10–15 minutes of what I called the 'business side' of their work, i.e., 'Are you up to date on court/review reports and other such organizational requirements?' That left me free for the remaining time to concentrate on how their emotions were affecting their decision-making.

I didn't know it at the time, but I later learnt that when thinking becomes infused with unregulated emotion – what is termed 'hot cognition' when excessive – then the ability to make sense of complex, often competing ideas and information is significantly impeded. (Readers familiar with Daniel Kahneman's (2011) notion of 'fast and slow thinking' will see some connections.) The relative weight I gave to the two key components of supervision, i.e., the 'work' and the 'worker', indicates, a 'both-and' logic rather than an 'either-or' configuration. We need a focus on relationships, at times to 'eclipse' paperwork, form-filling and unnecessary bureaucracy, to allow for genuine, relationship-based practice (but let's not forget that the right kind of recording and record-keeping is also important, for both practitioners and supervisors).

Over the past few years, I have been providing training for managers and supervisors, inviting them to think about ways of changing the organizational culture so that 'supervision' isn't seen as the sole responsibility of a 'supervisor'. As all professionals involved in child protection need regularly and routinely to side-step the problems associated with 'hot cognition', this means that supervision isn't something that can wait two to three weeks until 'formal supervision' takes place. Instead, it needs to be something that every team member can offer to their colleagues whenever it is needed. But, because they are also taken up with their own work, this kind of support needs to be restricted to a two, three or five-minute 'by the water cooler' activity, as distinct from a 20 or 30-minute 'counselling' session, as they simply don't have the time to do that. For it to work well, the practitioner needs to be very focused and precise – to avoid the 'verbal deluge' that emerged in David Wilkins' research when practitioners spoke in supervision about the families they were working with.

An example I give comes from the first episode of a BBC Two, three-part documentary series that followed child protection practitioners visiting and working with families (Mirzoeff, 2012). The example concerns a newly qualified social worker who, after a tricky visit, and on their return to the office, says, as they walked past the photocopier:

> Any new job is always scary. It's not nice to be shouted at. He can flip from second to second. I'm worried about my own practice, worried about what will happen if I see him next. And yes it gets into my dreams and into my subconscious where I don't want it to be. If I'm that worried about [dad], if I'm that scared, how does [child aged around three years] feel in this...?

(I should say at this point that, for me, this is an excellent example of a worker being very precise in the way they expressed their experience after the visit.)

In my view, their strong feelings arose because the father had said, rather directly, to them, 'Right...you might be a training social worker but what I am still fuming about is the way that you accused me on Friday.' The father then shortly after continues, 'You're out to do one thing...and I know you're out to do one thing and I'll repeat it now with the camera... You're out to wreck us.'

I ask participants to discuss in smaller groups what they would say to help the practitioner regulate or process their strong feelings.

I've done this with well over 4000 participants now, and there are three types of response that I hear when I visit each group.

First, they usually ask lots of questions, which ends up feeling like an interrogation, and/or they offer a lot of advice but without having sufficient knowledge of the background, etc. (this was precisely what the early pioneers of 'relationship skills research' also found).

Second, they say things like 'I know just how you feel' or 'I've often been in that situation – for example, "Last week..."' (here, the problem is that the worker is describing how *they* feel, but that isn't necessarily how *the worker in the film* feels).

Third, they engage in a kind of 'office banter' aimed at cheering up the worker but, given what they have just said, it may not strike the right note: they are likely to feel ignored, however well intentioned the banter might have been.

I then ask them to have another attempt but to try this time to find a form of words, 'so that the social worker will experience you trying to understand how *they* are feeling' (and not ask questions or give advice).

Most participants freely admit that they find this rather difficult. I then offer the following example to illustrate what I'm getting at: 'So...the prospect of having to work with him has left you apprehensive...even a bit nervous maybe...and perhaps it's starting to affect your confidence...' (Said tentatively and with curiosity, not certainty.)

I go on to explain that I used the word 'prospect' because the social worker had said '*if* I see him again'. Clearly, it's unlikely to be 'if'; it's almost certainly going to be 'when'. I add that I would gauge from their reply whether I was reasonably accurate, and if not, I would try and add something to correct my misperception. This example illustrates what was meant by 'saying something that tries to be helpful in two, three or five minutes'.

There's plenty of research available now that tells us that such simple attempts at marked empathy and 'gentle curiosity' can significantly help, as I put it, 'to centre the workers' emotional clay' (using the analogy of a potter's wheel, where unless the lump of clay is centred, not much else can happen; indeed, without it, the clay tends to fly off in all directions).

Within a more formalized 'supervision' session – either individually or in a group setting – I'd want to bring out how the worker did well to keep the child firmly at the centre of things when they said, 'If I'm that worried about [dad], if I'm that scared, how does [the child] feel in this...?' (bearing in mind that many Local Child Safeguarding Practice Review reports point out that child protection professionals haven't always managed to do this).

It emerges later in the episode of the documentary that the parents have lost seven babies, each of whom tragically died, either during pregnancy or during birth (or soon afterwards). So perhaps the social worker was picking up something about the father's state of mind when they noted, 'He can flip from second to second.' I've often wondered whether the practitioner may have subconsciously tuned in to feelings of loss and grief, which may be manifesting themselves in a dissociated way. If so, this would be an example of where supervision can become a powerful forum for the development of practice skills with the manager as 'practice leader' but *in partnership* with the professional.

By now, it won't have escaped the reader's notice that what I've been describing here is precisely what I meant earlier when I stressed the need for managers and supervisors to model with social workers the kind of support and emotional containment that they as practitioners need to offer family members.

This has been a whistle-stop tour of a complicated and nuanced area of leadership. Because it centrally concerns human relationships, often in situations when people are struggling, how could it be otherwise? But I hope this has raised some important questions that can, in turn, help social workers do their 'rocket science'.

> **REFLECTIONS**
>
> 1. Think back to some organizational changes in your area of work. Which of these have lasted in the medium to long term, and why do you think they did?
> 2. How does your organization help practitioners when they have just returned from a challenging visit, and do you think it is usually effective in the long run?
> 3. In your experience, what proportion of a supervision session is devoted to what might be called the 'business side' of the work?

References

Barlow, J., Fisher, J. D. and Jones, D. (2012) *Systematic Review of Models of Analysing Significant Harm.* Oxford: University of Oxford/Department for Education.

Dorsey, S., Mustillo, S. A., Farmer, E. M. Z. and Elbogen, E. (2008) 'Caseworker assessments of risk for recurrent maltreatment: Association with case-specific risk factors and re-reports.' *Child Abuse and Neglect 32*, 3, 377–391.

Ferguson, H., Warwick, L., Disney, T., Leigh, J., Singh Cooner, T. and Beddoe, L. (2022) 'Relationship-based practice and the creation of therapeutic change in long-term work: Social work as a holding relationship.' *Social Work Education 41*, 2, 209–227.

Forrester, D., Killian, M., Westlake, D. and Sheehan, L. (2020) 'Patterns of practice: An exploratory factor analysis of child and family social worker skills.' *Child and Family Social Work 25*, 1, 108–117.

Kahneman, D. (2011) *Thinking, Fast and Slow.* New York: Farrar, Strauss and Giroux.

Megele, C. (2015) *Psychosocial and Relationship-Based Practice.* St Albans: Critical Publishing.

Mirzoeff, S. (2012) *Protecting Our Children.* London: BBC. www.bbc.co.uk/webarchive/https%3A%2F%2Fwww.bbc.co.uk%2Fblogs%2Ftv%2F2012%2F01%2Fprotecting-our-children.shtml

Wilkins, D. (2017) 'Does reflective supervision have a future in English local authority child and family social work?' *Journal of Children's Services 12*, 2–3, 164–173.

• Chapter 14 •

AUTHENTIC LEADERSHIP

Yvette Stanley

> Yvette Stanley is Ofsted's National Director for Social Care and was previously Director for Children, Schools and Families at Merton Council. Yvette has held multiple leadership positions in the past and has more than 35 years of experience in children's services. In her current role, Yvette leads on the regulation of early years and social care provision as well as the inspection of children's social care, joint targeted inspections and Ofsted safeguarding work across remits.

Authentic leadership is a style of leadership that values honesty, transparency, sincerity and genuineness. Leaders who adopt this approach are likely to be successful in creating positive work environments and relationships. Such approaches are also more likely to inspire confidence, trust and loyalty within the organization, which in turn has a positive impact on the individuals and communities we serve.

I've been an advocate for authentic leadership for several years, and in this chapter, I outline my career journey to demonstrate its value and positive impact.

My career in children's service started three decades ago, when I worked in London's child guidance services. These services brought together professionals from a range of disciplines across health, social care and education, who worked with children who had experienced sexual abuse. Our work straddled the need to achieve best evidence through criminal prosecution with ongoing therapeutic interventions to support children of all ages.

In experiencing the very different professional cultures, legal frameworks and ways of working across team members, I started to think about the leadership needed for successful multi-disciplinary and partnership working. Years later, this thinking came again to the fore with the Every Child Matters green paper (HM Treasury, 2003) and the Children Act (2004), which enshrined the importance of multi-disciplinary partnership work at both strategic and child level.

Throughout my years as a director of children's services, delivering integrated services for children and families and then as Ofsted's national director, overseeing single and multi-agency inspections of safeguarding and care, getting the environment right for great multi-disciplinary and partnership practice to thrive has been front and centre of my thinking and leadership practice. I hope I have become an advocate for authenticity not just as an approach to support leadership across disciplines and partnership cultures but also as a foundation that resonates strongly with the values and discipline required for great social work practice.

At the start of my career, research on leadership was scant. So I looked for role models and learnt from those around me: 'to be or not to be' like them. I learnt positively from the inspirational, the diligent and the well prepared. I discovered I liked to work for people who were passionate about making a positive impact on children's lives. I learnt that a harsh or unfair word or poor behaviour from a leader is long remembered across the whole organization. I learnt that kindness, especially when giving a difficult message, will be paid back in buckets in loyalty and commitment to the organization. And most importantly, I learnt that the impact of all these attributes feeds through to the experiences of children and families and the communities we serve.

Leaders come to children's services from different professions involved with supporting children. We have differing professional cultures, languages and expectations, as well as differing personal perspectives and assumptions that we bring from our own roots and shoots.

I looked to see what I could garner from my professional network. I realized that common words – supervision, assessment, audit and risk – had very different interpretations. More importantly, I learnt that the culture and environment for both single professional and collective team needs *would require leaders who could serve the needs of each component part, as well as challenging elements of culture or practice that impeded a combined culture in which we could all thrive*. We needed to be adaptive, have a wide and versatile repertoire and to understand – and respond to – the professional as well as personal needs of our direct reports and wider staff.

These nimble and adaptive leadership requirements were particularly needed given the 'Team around the Child and Family' approach enshrined in Every Child Matters.

My next big foray into a multi-disciplinary world was as an assistant director commissioning and delivering integrated children's services.

As we came together at system and operational levels, I found that colleagues all had different perspectives on our decision-making and that this was based on the individual profession's cultural expectations and traditional hierarchies, which might not be recognized by 'outsiders'.

For example, two paediatricians could comfortably hold polarized positions, but if one of the clinicians was a nurse, the doctor's view generally prevailed. Schools had more embedded 'non-teacher-professionals' but occasionally when I visited a school there was still the option of two staffrooms at teatime: one for teaching and one for non-teaching staff. Social workers would challenge each other – but always felt more 'junior' to a headteacher or paediatrician. Still, the social workers were often left knitting together the conflicting views across the network, whilst holding the lion's share of risk.

Put simply for me, whatever discipline we started in, we come together in a common purpose to make the most difference we can for children and families. Building on that purpose gives a common platform for diverse professionals. Our personal purpose must be to do this as best we can. To do so we must be self-aware: cultivating our strengths, being conscious of our own 'need to improve' and knowing what support networks we need to be our resilient best selves.

Professionally diverse teams can find common cause in shared values. Being child-centred, family-focused, respectful and kind are key in our professional relationships, as well as essential for our direct work. We are authentic when we make those values transparent in all our interactions, large or small. Saying we put children front and centre is not as impactful as actually doing that each and every day. Showing conspicuous care to individual children is key. The journey to (all forms of) permanency has never been about meeting an adoption target; it is about delivering a loving stable home for a child or sibling group.

Building a relationship with a child, adult or a professional network requires empathy or heart. It means asking ourselves, 'What does this person or organization need from me? What can I give and how do I best articulate what I need from them?' These are the basics of any successful human relationships. The earliest languages started with 'I see you' and 'I hear you' as greetings. I would ask readers to consider the complementarity nature of authentic and relational leadership. Relational leadership values inclusion, empowerment, purposefulness and ethical behaviour. The relational approach which we value in our work with children and families also nests at the heart of our internal staffing and wider professional networks.

We serve diverse communities, and we serve them better when we reflect and respect that diversity, and when we honour each other's heritages and the journeys we have taken to arrive where we are today. Our narratives, human frailty and humility give people hope, contribute to a culture of internal learning and create the safe containing environment where 'Judgement of Solomon' decisions have to be made quickly and with the knowledge that hindsight might shed a different light and offer alternative solutions.

And why self-discipline? Bright ideas amount to nothing without disciplined thought and action to make stuff happen. Good social work needs us to follow through with the action we promise. We need to be highly organized and to constantly prioritize. Multi-disciplinary work needs reliable colleagues who follow up and follow through. Complexity needs rigour, determination and grip on all the moving parts.

So, my advice to aspirant leaders is that of authenticity. Authentic leaders are clear in their purpose and lead with their hearts as well as their heads. They are visible and visibly child-centred. They take tough decisions but deliver tough messages with kindness and respect.

They are present. They are willing to be challenged and will change opinions or strategies in the face of common sense or evidence. They do not let their egos get in the way of a better option. Their values are, however, a constant.

They understand their own journey, their strengths and frailties. They are willing to share these to support others' learning and to demonstrate their own. They are self-aware, not self-obsessed.

Authentic leaders serve through a combination of values-driven and relationship-based approaches. They align the heart and the head. A passion to make a difference is supported by disciplined thought and action. In the complex world of child protection, where risks are dynamic and certainty elusive, they promote learning by empowering those closest to the child, or with the subject expertise to help develop best-fit decision-making. Authentic leaders model listening, learning and the building of consensus. They establish long-term relationships that enable evidence-based and reality-checked decision-making, which makes a positive difference – for children, families, staff and partners.

I have been hugely fortunate to work with brilliant people who have shaped my authentic leadership journey. I am grateful to all those who have generously provided me with their timely insights, large and small, which have shaped my thinking and my practice. But of course, it is the children and families who teach us the most. They hold the mirror to our work as they share their experiences, reliving their pain or their dilemmas and painful choices, or absence of choices, that often reflect our impact and our limitations.

Our reflection and learning today supports better practice tomorrow. One of our key tasks as leaders is to leave better leaders behind us and to build the environment where the very best practice can thrive. If we are to leave our organizations, services and the children and families in a better place than when we arrived, we need to empower and give agency. As with our work with families, we 'work with' not, 'do to'.

My final word is on the importance of our support team. We can feed our own resilience by surrounding ourselves with a team who share our values and have similar aspirations. Honesty, transparency and kindness at the top creates an open and positive culture for work. This is what I consider to be authentic leadership.

REFLECTIONS

1. Does my value-led approach inhibit or embrace: co-production, common purpose or my purpose?
2. How much time and energy am I investing in building a trusted relational and inclusive approach in my team, service or partnership network?
3. Am I showing care about the right things? How would others answer that question about my areas of focus?

References

Children Act (2004) www.legislation.gov.uk/ukpga/2004/31/contents
HM Treasury (2003) *Every Child Matters.* London: The Stationery Office.

• Chapter 15 •

LEADERSHIP LITERACY

Reflections on Relational Leadership

Michael Preston-Shoot

> Professor Michael Preston-Shoot is Emeritus Professor of Social Work at the University of Bedfordshire and Independent Chair at Greenwich, Lewisham and Somerset Safeguarding Adults Boards. He is also the Joint Convenor of the National Network of SAB (Safeguarding Adults Board) Chairs.

Introduction

This chapter draws on the lived experience of one Safeguarding Adults Board (SAB) independent chair who has also been commissioned by other Boards to complete safeguarding adult reviews (SARs) or offer consultation on the development and review of their governance arrangements. He is one of the principal investigators of the first and second national thematic analyses of SARs (Preston-Shoot et al., 2020, 2024). He is also currently the joint convenor of the National Network for SAB Chairs. This lived experience of leadership in adult safeguarding policy and practice will be illustrated around the concept of literacy. Literacy here means particular knowledge and skill acquired from research, practice experience, professional training and feedback from people with lived experience of services.

Safeguarding Adults Boards

SABs in England were formally established in statute law by section 43 of the Care Act (2014). There are different legal rules for the governance of adult safeguarding in Wales and adult protection in Scotland. However, the basic purpose is the same across the three jurisdictions, namely to develop and ensure the effectiveness of how services prevent and protect people from abuse and neglect.

SABs have three statutory partners, namely the local authority, police and NHS integrated care boards. Other statutory and third sector organizations are invited partners. SABs have three statutory duties, namely to publish a strategic plan and an annual report, and to commission SARs where either the mandatory or the discretionary criteria in section 44 of the Care Act (2014) are met.

Section 43 describes SAB objectives as being to help and protect adults in cases of abuse and neglect by coordinating and ensuring the effectiveness of what each of its partners does. This might include the publication of policies, guidance and procedures, the promotion of multi-agency training and the commissioning of multi-agency practice audits and SARs.

SAB functions are further defined in statutory guidance (Department of Health and Social Care, 2023). SABs must establish links with other relevant partnerships, such as those responsible for community safety and safeguarding children. They should hold partners accountable for the quality, responsiveness and effectiveness of their adult safeguarding activity in preventing abuse and neglect (including self-neglect) and safeguarding adults at risk. Thus, Boards have important leadership, challenge, development, training, coordination and quality assurance roles in relation to inter-agency adult safeguarding arrangements (Braye and Preston-Shoot, 2020).

SAB effectiveness depends on the leadership that all members provide. Effective performance monitoring and review, and the embedding of learning from SARs and from audits for practice improvement and service development, will depend on the openness, transparency and trust within and between agencies, and on the ability of Board members to transcend representation of their own agency (*ibid.*).

Amongst the attitudes and skills needed to achieve positive outcomes are good interpersonal relationships, commitment to cross-sector and multi-agency working, open communication, positive challenge and the development of a shared vision (Preston-Shoot and Pratt, 2014).

SABs are not required to appoint independent chairs, although most do.

Chairs are responsible for ensuring SAB compliance with its statutory duties and for facilitating identification and accomplishment of locally agreed priorities in a strategic plan.

SAB partners have a duty to cooperate in order that the partnership can complete its statutory duties (sections 6, 7 and 45 of the Care Act, 2014). Statutory guidance (Department of Health and Social Care, 2023) encourages partner agencies to provide resources to support the SAB's work but levels of financial support vary widely. Independent chairs cannot instruct SAB partners to contribute. Their role is to promote and facilitate a collective approach to preventing and safeguarding adults from abuse and neglect. They must ensure appropriate engagement with local communities and people who use services. The role involves collaborative leadership, offering advice, support, encouragement and constructive challenge, and holding all partners to account for how they are complying with their duties to safeguarding adults at risk (*ibid.*).

SAB independent chairs therefore have authority of position but little if any formal power. The relevance of their prior experience might support the establishment of their authority but it has to be negotiated rather than assumed and is ultimately dependent on the quality of the relationships that they are able to develop with senior leaders across statutory and third sector agencies, and with practitioners, operational managers and community representatives.

Building blocks for relational leadership

SABs are organizational entities where multi-agency partnership requirements have been grafted onto single agency structures and so rely on partner commitment and cooperation. Standards and principles of good governance require Board members to have sufficient seniority to provide strategic leadership in the development and monitoring of safer safeguarding practice, demonstrating integrity, selflessness, accountability, openness, honesty and learning-focused leadership (Nolan Committee on Standards in Public Life, 1995; OPM and CIPFA, 2004; Audit Commission, 2005; Braye, Orr and Preston-Shoot, 2012). Leadership is, therefore, everyone's business.

To establish and maintain a culture that mirrors these standards and principles, and to be effective champions of practice improvement and service development, in a context of the increasing breadth, volume and complexity of adult safeguarding, demands the ability to establish authority for leadership and thence to build collaborative, trustful and candid relationships. It involves negotiation, mindful that each partner will have its own imperatives, staff recruitment and retention issues, and financial constraints, and that independent chairs have little positional power (Preston-Shoot 2012; Preston-Shoot and Pratt, 2014).

Several building blocks for establishing authority and building collaborative, relational leadership are essential, and these include:

Domain 1: Knowledge

Some literacies belong to the knowledge domain (Lang, Little and Cronen, 1990). To understand how services should work together and to promote effective practice, policy for and management of practice to prevent or to protect individuals from abuse/neglect, knowledge of law and safeguarding are fundamental.

Legal literacy

Independent chairs must ensure that SABs comply with their legal duties. In England that requires knowledge of the requirements in sections 43 and 44 of the Care Act (2014) and in the statutory guidance (Department of Health and Social Care, 2023). SABs themselves can be held to account. Their decision-making is open to challenge through judicial review and investigation by the Local Government and Social Care Ombudsman, hence the importance of legal literacy to ensure compliance with statutory duties and adherence to the standards for decision-making enshrined in administrative law.

These standards require that decision-making: is lawful, reasonable and rational; is timely and consultative, and takes account of all relevant considerations; considers whether to exercise discretion; and provides recorded reasons for decisions. Additionally, as part of their mandate to seek assurance about the effectiveness of adult safeguarding, SAB chairs require knowledge of the law relating to adult safeguarding. In England that includes section 42 of the Care Act (2014), alongside powers and duties in the Mental Capacity Act (2005), Mental Health Acts (1983/2007), Human Rights Act (1998) and Equality Act (2010).

There will also be occasions when a basic knowledge of other legislation will be helpful in seeking assurance that statutory services are complying with their legal duties to prevent or safeguard people from modern slavery, domestic abuse, financial abuse, discriminatory abuse, neglect, self-neglect and organizational abuse.

Safeguarding literacy

Research, feedback from people with lived experience of adult safeguarding services, SAR findings and contributions from practitioners and managers across health, housing and social care have enabled the development of an evidence base for positive practice. Examples of this evidence base include adult safeguarding and homelessness (Preston-Shoot, 2020), discriminatory abuse (Mason, 2023), self-neglect (Preston-Shoot, 2019) and transitional safeguarding (Preston-Shoot, Cocker and Cooper, 2022). With knowledge of 'what good looks like', SAB chairs will be better able to scrutinize performance data, to comment reflectively and critically on SAR recommendations and to hold services to account.

Ethical literacy

Adult safeguarding is replete with dilemmas where the right thing to do will not always be obvious and will possibly be contested. There will be questions about when health, social care and other services should intervene, and about how to balance a person's autonomy and self-determination (or the right to a private and family life) with a duty of care and a duty to prevent and/or protect individuals from harm (or the right to life). To decide whether and how to intervene requires ethical reasoning. Governance of adult safeguarding, reviewing individual cases and seeking assurance through audits, reports and monitoring of performance data will also encounter these same dilemmas.

Leadership here demands a critically reflective approach to sense-making rather than simple acceptance of principles. It requires the ability to wrestle with uncertainty and ambiguity, to manage competing perspectives, to interrogate beliefs and assumptions and to reach for a position of safer uncertainty (Mason, 2019).

Domain 2: Explanation

Adult safeguarding is multi-dimensional, multi-factorial, multi-agency and multi-disciplinary. It might be termed a wicked problem (Grint, 2008), since adult safeguarding practice involves uncertainty about what is happening, generates different explanations or alternative perspectives and, therefore, stimulates debates about how best to respond. Repetitive SAR findings illustrate the apparent intractability of challenges, uncertainties and ambiguities in adult safeguarding where the right responses are not self-evident and where a collaborative response is needed (*ibid.*).

Management and governance of adult safeguarding reflects this context.

To build relationships for collaborative practice, and management and governance of practice, requires leadership that helps to make sense of this context in order to facilitate system change. 'Safeguarding is everyone's business' is another way of acknowledging that the challenges inherent in adult safeguarding are system-wide, neither caused nor resolved by one agency acting alone. Change depends on collaboration and relationships.

Relational literacy

Leadership is dialogic, involving exchange and debate, support and challenge. Leadership embodies an investigatory and inquisitive mindset. Its purpose is to promote individual and collective reflection about adult safeguarding practice in a multi-agency and multi-disciplinary context.

SAB chairs ideally demonstrate appreciative and authoritative questioning and curiosity. The relationships they establish should enable them to manage their accountability 'upwards' with the local authority chief executive, ultimately responsible for their continued appointment, and other senior leaders of the statutory partners to whom they must report annually. However, their accountability also extends 'downwards' to practitioners, operational managers and people with lived experience of adult safeguarding, to whom they are accountable for the quality of provision.

Finally, their accountability extends 'sideways' to the connections and collaborative relationships that SAB chairs are able to establish and maintain with Board members and which are fundamental to knowing about and improving adult safeguarding practice.

Psychodynamic and systemic literacy

The breadth, uncertainty, anxiety, risk and complexity inherent in adult safeguarding requires an understanding of what happens within and between workers, and within and between organizational systems.

Independent chairs must be able to think and act systemically when seeking to understand practice and how it can be improved. They must simultaneously pay attention to the emotional impact of uncertainty, dilemmas and discomfort, and the levels and impact of individual and organizational emotions, such as anxiety. Leadership in this context involves being able to tolerate one's own and other people's discomfort, sadness, outrage and disappointment – whatever the emotions are within and between SAB members, prompted by the human stories they witness, especially through SARs.

Organizational literacy

The chair's prior experience might have been at different levels within one of the statutory partners and/or drawn from outside of health, social care or uniform services. Their leadership requires that they move beyond their personal, professional identity. Leading systemically means adopting a position of neutrality (Preston-Shoot and Agass, 1990). SAB chairs do not align or identify themselves with any one of the Board's partners. Practice then is characterized by balance in its focus on services and in its goal to improve the quality of adult safeguarding practice through developing the relationships between services. They should recognize the impact of workload pressures, staff shortages, resource limitations and organizational cultures. Organizational cultures, systems and expectations, and individual and collective fears, can create conditions where negative delay, error and poor practice are more likely. Alongside development days, subgroups and project planning, conversations are ongoing and safeguarding themes are revisited for assurance, practice improvement and service development.

Emotional literacy

The chair should understand that how we are with people matters. Leadership involves acting with integrity, generosity, courage, compassion, resilience and respect in the face of strong emotions. Once again, balance is evident, namely passion with fairness, understanding and analysis with advocacy. They are willing to challenge decisions and escalate concerns. The chair has the ability to question the stories we tell ourselves, such as narratives about people experiencing homelessness and/or substance misuse. They can contain and reflect on, rather than act out, stress, anxiety, fear, uncertainty and blame and the impact of emotions. The chair should have the resilience and courage to ask themselves and others difficult questions and to find right-enough answers.

Domain 3: Aesthetics

The aesthetic domain (Lang et al., 1990) encourages those involved to critique current systems and to reflect on system design that captures our ambitions for effective adult safeguarding.

Values literacy

SAB leadership sometimes involves overcoming the silencing of stories and the invisibility of voices, recognizing structural oppression and powerlessness, for example racism in mental health provision, discriminatory abuse in service provision for people with learning disabilities or coercion and controlling behaviour in domestic abuse. It is about making known unheard stories, untold narratives and unknown experiences, for example through SARs (Preston-Shoot, 2023). It is about making uncertainty safer, about holding on until movement is a possibility, about being a home. It is about being a champion for those who feel lost, lonely, traumatized, and hopeless and in despair; for those who are marginalized and powerless in society. It is the telling of human stories that might promote transformational, attitudinal practice and sometimes policy and legislative change.

Political literacy
Leadership requires a wide-angle lens. Adult safeguarding operates within, and is not independent of, a legal, policy and financial context from which it derives its legitimacy and authority (Yu, 2015). Adult safeguarding can only be understood in its context, including the impact on services of austerity and emphasis on case management rather than relationship-based practice. Adult safeguarding is about social justice and human rights. The lack of a national focus, failing to explore the connections between local experience and the national context, limits any conversation about political accountability with government concerning the impact of economic and social policy on service provision and people's lives (Cambridge, 2004). Adult safeguarding, to be a geography of hope, is political.

Future focused literacy
The chair's leadership aims to be transformative and involves capturing what matters deeply in human and professional life, within a social justice, equalities and human-rights framework. This includes questioning and challenging, facilitating thoughtfulness and stimulating a capacity to imagine, explore possibilities and envision.

Leadership learning points

Leadership is, indeed, everyone's business. Accordingly, Board members will also draw on the various types of literacy just described. Responsibility does not rest solely on the shoulders of the independent chair. However, independent chairs have a particular role in creating space for different contributions to emerge across the three domains – knowledge, explanation and aesthetics. They have a particular role in shaping and maintaining the

SAB as a heterarchy (Grint, 2008) – a non-hierarchical set of relationships where knowledge, skills and experience can be shared.

Creating this space and culture involves leadership that guides, enabling voices to be heard, or acknowledging, holding and containing difficult truths, or being curious about the stories being told or not told. It involves leadership that facilitates, enabling concerns to be articulated and reflections to be shared. It is leadership as a critical friend, questioning whether the conditions exist for change to occur and for pursuit of common goals rather than just single agency imperatives.

The value of independence lies in the space that non-alignment with any one agency or service creates. Using the medium of interpersonal relationships, and a collaborative and participative style, leadership is curious, inquisitive, questioning and observational – exploring and commenting on the effectiveness of multi-agency partnership working at strategic and operational levels, acknowledging complexity and reaching for new possibilities through the contributions of Board partners. In systemic terms, this represents a meta position (Preston-Shoot and Agass, 1990), finding a vantage point from which to promote exploration and appropriate responses to the challenges presented within adult safeguarding.

REFLECTIONS

1. Which of the literacies described above do you recognize from your own experience of leadership?
2. What has been your own experience of leadership in multi-disciplinary, multi-agency settings?
3. Having read this chapter, what might you take into your own leadership practice?

References

Audit Commission (2005) *Governing Partnerships: Bridging the Accountability Gap.* London: Audit Commission.

Braye, S. and Preston-Shoot, M. (2020) 'Adult Safeguarding.' In S. Braye and M. Preston-Shoot (eds) *The Care Act 2014: Wellbeing in Practice* (pp.81–97). London: Learning Matters/Sage.

Braye, S., Orr, D. and Preston-Shoot, M. (2012) 'The governance of adult safeguarding: Findings from research.' *Journal of Adult Protection 14*, 2, 55–72.

Cambridge, P. (2004) 'Abuse Inquiries as Learning Tools for Social Care Organisations.' In N. Stanley and J. Manthorpe (eds) *The Age of Inquiry: Learning and Blaming in Health and Social Care* (pp.231–254). London: Routledge.

Department of Health and Social Care (2023) Care and Support Statutory Guidance. www.gov.uk/government/publications/care-act-statutory-guidance/care-and-support-statutory-guidance

Grint, K. (2008) 'Wicked problems and clumsy solutions.' *Clinical Leader 1*, 2, 11–25.

Lang, P., Little, M. and Cronen, V. (1990) 'The systemic professional: Domains of action and the question of neutrality.' *Human Systems 1*, 1, 34–49.

Mason, B. (2019) 'Revisiting safe uncertainty: Six perspectives for clinical practice and the assessment of risk.' *Journal of Family Therapy 41*, 3, 343–356.

Mason, K. (2023) 'Harassment and slurs or epistemic injustice? Interrogating discriminatory abuse through safeguarding adult review analysis.' *Journal of Adult Protection 25*, 5, 254–265.

Nolan Committee on Standards in Public Life (1995) *The Seven Principles of Public Life.* London: The Stationery Office.

OPM and CIPFA (2004) *The Good Governance Standard for Public Services.* London: Independent Commission on Good Governance in Public Services.

Preston-Shoot, M. (2012) 'Local Safeguarding Children Boards: Faith, Hope and Evidence.' In M. Blyth and E. Solomon (eds) *Effective Safeguarding for Children and Young People: What Next after Munro?* (pp.25–50). Bristol: Policy Press.

Preston-Shoot, M. (2019) 'Self-neglect and safeguarding adult reviews: Towards a model of understanding facilitators and barriers to best practice.' *Journal of Adult Protection 21*, 4, 219–234.

Preston-Shoot, M. (2020) *Adult Safeguarding and Homelessness: A Briefing on Positive Practice.* London: Local Government Association and Association of Directors of Adult Social Services.

Preston-Shoot, M. (2023) 'Human stories about self-neglect: Told, untold, untellable and unheard narratives in safeguarding adult reviews.' *Journal of Adult Protection 25*, 6, 321–338.

Preston-Shoot, M. and Agass, D. (1990) *Making Sense of Social Work: Psychodynamics, Systems and Practice.* London: Macmillan.

Preston-Shoot, M. and Pratt, M. (2014) 'Symbolic Half-Measures? On Local Safeguarding Children Boards, Their Contributions and Challenges.' In M. Blyth (ed.) *Moving on from Munro: Improving Children's Services* (pp.159–182). Bristol: Policy Press.

Preston-Shoot, M., Braye, S., Preston, O., Allen, K. and Spreadbury, K. (2020) *Analysis of Safeguarding Adult Reviews April 2017–March 2019: Findings for Sector Led Improvement.* London: Local Government Association and Directors of Adult Social Services.

Preston-Shoot, M., Braye, S., Stacey, H., Doherty, C., et al. (2024) *Second National Analysis of Safeguarding Adult Reviews April 2019–March 2023. Findings for Sector Led Improvement.* London: Local Government Association and Directors of Adult Social Services.

Preston-Shoot, M., Cocker, C. and Cooper, A. (2022) 'Learning from safeguarding adult reviews about transitional safeguarding: Building an evidence-base.' *Journal of Adult Protection 24*, 2, 90–101.

Yu, N. (2015) 'Conclusion: Rights, Justice, the Law and Extra Legal Action.' In N. Yu and D. Mandell (eds) *Subversive Action: Extra Legal Practice for Social Justice* (pp.165–176). Ontario: Wilfrid Laurier University Press.

• Chapter 16 •

LEADERSHIP FOR ENVIRONMENTAL SUSTAINABILITY

Godfred Boahen and Sarah Range

Dr Godfred Boahen is Bi-Borough Head of Service for Learning Disability and Autism, Westminster and Royal Borough of Kensington and Chelsea. After gaining a degree in Politics, Philosophy and Economics at St Anne's College (University of Oxford), Godfred trained as a Social Worker at the University of York. He holds a PhD in learning disability and ethnicity and is widely published in the areas of social work leadership and practice including poverty and anti-racist supervision.

Sarah Range has worked within adult social care since the mid-1990s when she started her career as a care worker. She holds both a bachelor's and a master's degree in Social Work and has practised in America and in the UK in both the not-for-profit and local authority settings. She has a passion for social justice and compassionate leadership. Her chapter is dedicated to N and E.

Introduction

Writing as senior managers in social care services, we argue that to address environmental sustainability, sector leaders need to acknowledge their own 'vulnerability' (Minor, 2022; see also Buzzi and Megele, Chapter 2 of this book).

We – citizens, staff and leaders – all *see* the emerging impact of climate change. It is now real. What previously appeared as distant technical debates amongst 'experts' *feels* palpable, immediate and unstoppable. Leaders will also experience fear, anxiety and powerlessness that this existential challenge elicits (Vercammen, Oswald and Lawrance, 2023). However, this may be more acute in adult social care (ASC) leadership because while we are not subject experts, we are required to find organizational 'solutions'.

In this chapter, we reflect on why, of all our operational and strategic responsibilities, environmental sustainability feels like such an intractable area. We suggest that while the climate emergency might seem insurmountable and provoke a range of emotions, there are organizationally practical options for local authority leaders to reprioritize environmental sustainability while meeting financial sustainability objectives.

Environmental sustainability in adult social care

It's estimated that the economic value of ASC is £50.3 billion. This 'is a bigger sector than electricity and power, water and waste management and twice as big as agriculture' (Skills for Care, 2021, p.1). The industries cited in this quote have significant environmental impact. That social care is bigger throws the need for its leaders to have unrelenting focus on sustainability into sharp focus.

However, the environment may not feature as prominently as other issues for ASC leaders. Budgets, improvement or political accountability may *feel* more immediate for organizational sustainability. Senior leaders across most sectors adjudicate between complex and competing choices, which they are required to accord the same level of importance. But within social care, environmental sustainability seems to be relegated to the background. For example, ASC has a duty to ensure the safety and wellbeing of vulnerable people at risk of abuse or neglect, and this may involve frequent car trips by staff to monitor people's wellbeing. This creates environmental impact and, arguably, presents a conflict between the ethical duties to protect the environment and statutory requirement to keep people safe. While the law requires us to prioritize the latter above the former, as leaders we need to acknowledge the tension between the two and operationalize both, thus resolving the apparent trade-offs between keeping people safe and/or environmental sustainability.

Meanwhile, as we (re)prioritize strategic imperatives, the already convincing evidence base about the impact of the 'climate emergency' strengthens, and we all observe it impacting service delivery in unexpected ways. For instance, 'weather-related absenteeism' (Young and Bergsen, 2020, p.4), in which unusually cold or hot periods impact on the ability of staff to get to work, also affects social care. Maintaining services during adverse weather events, which can be experienced for weeks or months rather than days, can lead to unsustainable working hours with negative effects on the workforce. As leaders, we need to build resilient organizations and are required by law to develop operational plans for maintaining service in this era of climate change (Department for Environment, Food and Rural Affairs, 2024).

Climate change therefore provokes contrary emotions in us in our leadership roles. Privately, we live with the same fears, worries and powerlessness as most people. Professionally, we are required to discharge statutory responsibilities on environmental sustainability, and we also wish to prioritize this, but policy and budgetary situations push us in a different direction. We need to act differently, and to do so, we can start by thinking about our leadership style.

Sustainability and adult social care: recognizing leaders' vulnerabilities as strengths

Increasingly, leadership theories have moved away from 'Great Man' models in which the leader is cast as the person with all the answers. The 'Great Man' is also implicit in policy emphasis on 'transformation', which conjures up the image of a visionary who has worked up answers that less enlightened followers cannot fathom (see Boahen and Wiles, 2018 for a discussion of leadership models in ASC).

However, this stoical approach to leading may not be effective regarding the ongoing climate emergency. This is because while the evidence base is strong, the 'solutions' are contested and contextual, and it requires leaders to manage citizens' fear about the existential consequences of climate change.

Weintrobe (2012) has suggested three emotional responses in the understanding of climate change: (i) denialism, a campaign of sustained misinformation; (ii) negation, denying the existence of something that is; (iii) disavowal, the acknowledgement of the existence of what is but the minimizing of its significance.

Arguably (iii) is more applicable in ASC. While recognizing the existential threat of the climate emergency, we don't always consciously consider and try to mitigate the impact of our professional decisions on climate change.

More recently, convincing research shows that leaders who show vulnerability are better able to connect and develop more effective solutions and collaboration with their staff. Lopez (2018, p.4) defines vulnerability in leadership as:

> *a willingness to be transparent and emotionally exposed in relationship with another individual, with the possibility of being hurt or attacked*. For example, a leader could share their feelings of fear when taking a new risk, or share what it feels like to move past prior failure and take on a bold new vision. *Vulnerability is considered a choice leaders make, and can only be experienced in communion with someone else*. (Emphasis added; see also Buzzi and Megele, Chapter 2 of this book)

This steers us towards more relational models of leadership in which we accept that, as leaders, we do not have the answers because we are not experts in climate science. From this position, we work with others (staff, sector leaders, government) to co-produce solutions. Through this, we can build organizational trust and increase the propensity of staff to independently problem-solve because they feel psychologically safe in the organization (Academy for Sustainable Innovation, 2023). Lopez (2018) argues that they associate vulnerability with courage, authenticity and trustworthiness, meaning that they are more likely to adopt the approach of leaders who demonstrate that model in their roles.

We suggest that Lopez's work cited above, in relation to sustainability in adult social care, implies:

- leaders acknowledging their own fears about the existential threat of climate change

- leaders being transparent about their lack of expertise and registering that this might make them relegate it on the list of organizational priorities

- leaders working consciously to overcome the above by building alliances with staff and colleagues to find solutions.

Of course, this approach to leadership has potential drawbacks. For instance, others may perceive a leader who acknowledges their lack of expertise as incompetent. It can also be seen as merely performative if a display of vulnerability is not accompanied by actions to build solution-oriented collaborations (Browne, Danely and Rosenow, 2021). So what are some of the ways we can begin to address environmental sustainability in our organizations and operations?

Doing things differently on sustainability in social care: practical ideas for leadership

Social care leaders are uniquely placed to create a sustainable impact on our environment. If underpinned by an ethos of increased productivity and involvement of people who use services, and/or their carers, this has additional benefits of delivering efficiencies and budget savings. We develop some of these themes further below.

Sustainability through prevention

Social care legislation requires local authorities to 'consider whether or how the person's needs could be reduced or other needs delayed from arising. Effective interventions at the right time can stop needs from escalating, and help people maintain their independence for longer' (Department of Health and Social Care, 2014). Prevention contributes positively to environmental sustainability because meeting increased needs is likely to require use of more resources. So making prevention a core part of delivery enables some mitigation of unnecessary increases in the environmental impact of operations, whilst also entailing lower financial costs.

Prevention can be achieved through a more joined-up approach to sharing information between partners and further structural integration. Also, enabling people to live in the community for as long as possible can delay the need for more resource-intensive services, such as residential and domiciliary care (The Kings Fund, 2024). This combination can enhance environmental *and* budget sustainability.

The prevention agenda also applies to the operational aspect of ASC. In our operational leadership, we can work to streamline processes to enhance efficiency. For example, we can encourage staff to offer digital technology, to enable people to keep themselves safe whilst at home and to reduce the carbon footprint associated with care and support. This might mean, for example, the use of an alarm to remind people to take their medication or to alert for assistance in the case of a fall.

Environmentally sustainable care and support provision

The Department of Health and Social Care (2024) suggests streamlining social care assessments of need to make them more commensurate to the level of need. Organizations can introduce environmentally sustainable assessments and provision through:

- enhancing citizen choice and control by asking people how they want us to consider sustainability in our engagement with them

- increasing use of technology-enabled care

- reducing unnecessary travel to conduct face-to-face visits where tech-enabled assessments of care needs can lead to similar outcomes

- meeting corporate plan objectives to be more operationally efficient, thereby reducing the overall use of resources in discharging their statutory duties to meet eligible needs.

- empowering staff to use their initiatives to reduce their carbon footprint during assessments of care needs.

Emergency preparedness

Business Continuity Plans (BCPs) have a role in the support of environmentally sustainable practice, as they identify and plan for short-term and long-term environmental emergencies. These plans should consider the risks of climate change associated with natural disasters, such as storms, flooding, fire, snow and the impact of extreme temperatures, whilst ensuring that people in vulnerable circumstances and their staff are not adversely and avoidably impacted.

Leaders can work internally and with partners to develop robust environmental sustainability policies to govern the responses of our systems. All BCPs that are developed can be informed by individual organizational environmental sustainability policies and consider:

- modelling of how the climate crisis might impact on demand and delivery of services in an emergency

- how local communities can be galvanized to support resilience programmes at speed and with impact

- the geographical nature of the local authority – for instance, the rural or urban makeup of the community – and the sensitivity of the transport infrastructure to extreme weather events

- how to minimize the carbon footprint of provision whilst responding to an emergency.

Increasing workforce capabilities in sustainability

Organizational leaders have a golden opportunity to increase the skills and knowledge of our workforce in sustainability issues. Murowe (2023) suggests that all social care practitioners should ask themselves, 'What can I do to make my practice more environmentally sustainable?' Picking up this challenge, we can ensure that spaces are provided for staff to critically reflect on their environmental footprint. This would provoke practitioners to take ownership of the task at hand to minimize their carbon footprint in their practice. However, we also realize that, as organizational leaders, we need to provide the appropriate operational and physical infrastructure. The box below offers some of the many ways we can role-model and advocate for environmental sustainability.

- As leaders, we lead by example (Mortlock, 2023). We can articulate the case for sustainability and advocate for and adhere to green initiatives in the workplace.

- We can role-model and 'nudge' practitioners to use public transport as much as is practicable in their professional activities such as home visits.

- We can champion the use of technology to minimize the footprint of care provision.

- Audit and quality assurance processes can collect service user feedback to assess whether support plans that include the use of outdoor spaces have a positive impact on wellbeing.

- The continuing professional development that we endorse can offer opportunities to cover the psychosocial benefits of environmentally friendly interventions to improve wellbeing.

- Eco-advocacy can be a discussion point within the social care practice relationship at the supervisory level with our staff as well as part of a fundamental discussion with the people we work with.

- We can ensure awareness and adoption of the principles of green prescribing, in which the importance of and need for green outdoor spaces in the creation of care and support plans is recognized, and we can encourage them to be introduced at all levels of our organizations.

- We can work with commissioners to ensure that all contracts, from back-office function to carer transport and the delivery of care, include deliverables tied to the eco-agenda.

- We can actively and overtly support our eco-green staff forums. We can lend visible leadership to enable staff to contribute proactively to our community and demonstrate inter-organizational activism and championship.

- We can encourage our workforce to consider green options, use pool bikes and cars and be aware of subsidized/incentivized or interest-free loans for trains/buses.

- We can advocate for the introduction of incentives for staff who choose sustainable travel or for those who drive electric vehicles.

- Our organizations can increase their use of recyclable stationery and eco-friendly, biodegradable care products.

- We can impact on contractual arrangements, e.g., where feasible, requiring organizations to recycle personal protective equipment and workwear.

- Working with our information, communication and technology teams, we can champion the use of eco-friendly software (such as search engines that plant trees to offset carbon).

Conclusion

Recognizing that climate change is already impacting directly on our professional identity, on the 'demand' for social care services and on the sector's operations is perhaps the first step towards achieving greater environmental sustainability. We may feel intensely vulnerable about the existential threat posed by climate change yet, for a variety of reasons, consciously or unconsciously avoid considering our impact on climate change and how to reduce our carbon footprint. At times, this may be due to the immediacy and persistence of budgetary pressures and increasing demand that have sometimes appeared as priority existential concerns. However, as suggested earlier in this chapter, environmental and financial sustainability can go hand in hand, and some of the suggested actions in the preceding section offer the opportunity for reprioritizing environmental sustainability and incorporating this agenda into our work.

> **REFLECTIONS**
>
> 1. In what way does climate change and the need for sustainability feature in the organizational planning for your service?
> 2. What emotions arise for you when you consider the impact of climate change?
> 3. How can you encourage and support practical consideration of sustainability within your organization?

References

Academy for Sustainable Innovation (2023) The Role of Brave Leadership in Inspiring Climate Action. https://sustainableinnovation.academy/the-role-of-brave-leadership-in-inspiring-climate-action

Boahen, G. and Wiles, F. (2018) *Professionalism and Self-management: Social Work Skills in Practice*. London: Open University Press.

Browne, V., Danely, J. and Rosenow, D. (eds) (2021) *Vulnerability and the Politics of Care: Transdisciplinary.* British Academy Conference Proceedings Series. Oxford: Oxford University Press.

Department for Environment, Food and Rural Affairs (2024) Third National Adaptation Programme (NAP3). www.gov.uk/government/publications/third-national-adaptation-programme-nap3

Department of Health and Social Care (2014) Care and Support Statutory Guidance. www.gov.uk/government/publications/care-act-statutory-guidance/care-and-support-statutory-guidance

Department of Health and Social Care (2024) Proportionate Assessment Approaches in Adult Social Care. www.gov.uk/government/publications/proportionate-assessment-approaches-in-adult-social-care

Lopez, S. O. (2018) 'Vulnerability in leadership: The power of the courage to descend.' *Industrial-Organizational Psychology Dissertations 16*. https://digitalcommons.spu.edu/iop_etd/16

Minor, N. W. (2022) 'Followership and the Development of Future Leadership: A Narrative Study of Leaders and Vulnerability.' Doctoral dissertation, University of Charleston-Beckley.

Mortlock, J. (2023) 'Leadership, Engagement and Motivation.' In *Organisational Psychology* (pp.48–67). London: Routledge.

Murowe, T. (2023) 'Does Sustainability Have a Place in Social Work?' In T. Moore (ed.) *Principles of Practice by Principal Social Workers* (pp.83–93). St Albans: Critical Publishing.

Skills for Care (2021) *The Value of the Adult Social Care Market*. Leeds: Skills for Care. www.skillsforcare.org.uk/Adult-Social-Care-Workforce-Data/Workforce-intelligence/documents/The-value-of-adult-social-care-in-England-FINAL-report.pdf

The Kings Fund (2024) Key Facts and Figures about Adult Social Care. https://www.kingsfund.org.uk/audio-video/key-facts-figures-adult-social-care

Vercammen, A., Oswald, T. and Lawrance, E. (2023) 'Psycho-social factors associated with climate distress, hope and behavioural intentions in young UK residents.' *PLOS Global Public Health 3*, 8, e0001938.

Weintrobe, S. (2012) 'The Difficult Problem of Anxiety in Thinking about Climate Change.' In *Engaging with Climate Change* (pp.33–47). London: Routledge.

Young, S. and Bergsen, A. M. (2020) *Delivering Social Care in a Changing Climate*. Edinburgh: ClimateXChange. www.climatexchange.org.uk/wp-content/uploads/2023/09/cxc-delivering-social-care-in-a-changing-climate-june-2020.pdf

• Chapter 17 •

LEADERSHIP AND BLAME

Sharon Shoesmith

> Dr Sharon Shoesmith was Director of Children's Services for Haringey in 2007 at the time of the death of Peter Connelly, also known as 'Baby P', having been one of Her Majesty's Inspectors (HMI) with Ofsted. In her book *Learning from Baby P*, she carries out a dispassionate analysis of the events which followed Peter Connelly's death, documenting the responses of the media, politicians and the public, and exploring the psychological and emotional responses to such horrifying cases of familial child homicide and how the climate of fear and blame which follows such tragedies can lead to negative consequences for other children at risk of harm and for the social workers striving to protect them.

Introduction

This chapter is concerned with the leadership of directors of children's services (DCSs) in local authorities, with a specific focus on child protection.

First, I argue that the challenging context of leading children's services is neglected, especially the impact of multi-agency working, public perception and the interdependence of the media and politicians, or 'mediated politics'.

Second, to illustrate my argument, I draw upon the case of Peter, known in public as 'Baby P', who was 16 months old when he became the victim of familial child homicide.

Lastly, I explore how leaders of children's services might seek to overcome some of the challenges they face which may benefit the social work profession as a whole and the children they seek to protect.

1. The challenging context of children's services

The literature on the leadership of children's services focuses on the importance of shared values, professional empowerment and egalitarianism, all worthy aspects of relational leadership, but fails to engage with the challenges of the role.

The UK regulator Ofsted is a good example, describing successful leaders as 'open, honest and collaborative...driven by a strong moral base informed by solid professional knowledge' (Ofsted, 2015). Other significant contributors regard leadership as critical to good social work practice but with little in-depth analysis of the challenges leaders face (Laming, 2009; Munro, 2011). Haworth, Millar and Schaub (2018, p.19) get a little closer when they suggest that modern social work takes place in a 'complex and embattled context'.

In a day-to-day context, I argue that DCSs and their teams operate in the 'shadow of blame' resulting from public perception of social workers shaped and promoted by mediated politics (Jones, 2014; Leedham, 2022; Shoesmith, 2016, 2023; Warner, 2013, 2015).

DCSs over many decades, perhaps uniquely, have found themselves at the centre of widespread moral outrage when shocking cases of familial child homicide become the focus of intense political and media attention. Most often such outrage has no basis in evidence of gross misconduct, but it routinely ends professional careers. Notions of 'public accountability' have emerged, perhaps exclusively for DCSs, roughly translated as: 'We know you are not guilty, but you just have to go to bring an end to the public opprobrium.'

In this context, the ability of leaders to take an honest and robust stance, as opposed to a defensive acceptance of blame, and survive in their roles, is fraught with difficulty. Andrew Cooper, the late Professor of Social Work at London's Tavistock Clinic, offers a way of understanding the blaming of social workers. He suggests that 'we know children are harmed and abused but we cannot face it. The pain of knowing [that it happens] is too great... the perceived incompetence of social workers then functions as a defence for society...against having to tolerate knowledge of what is bad' (Cooper 2010, p.10).

He further suggests that society has no discourse to communicate such emotionally indigestible facts of child murder or torture (Cooper, 2014). At its core is the denial of what adults, especially mothers, are capable of. Such denial, with the encouragement of the mediated politics, results in punitive populism in which 'the public' takes up a hard-hitting and often aggressive stance towards social workers, rejecting evidence and expert opinion in favour of demanding the name of who is to blame.

Under the Children Act (2004), DCSs and their teams work in partnership with police and health professionals to protect children. These sovereign bodies have different roles, responsibilities and accountabilities, with the DCS, in a statutory role, carrying the main responsibility for the protection of children. For DCSs, it is in effect responsibility and accountability without power over the quality of work of other agencies. When things go wrong the role of partners is overlooked, allowing them to actively avoid criticism and loss of reputation as public opprobrium focuses on social workers (Jones, 2014; Shoesmith, 2016, 2023). Blaming social workers has, over many decades, become a habitual response devoid of reason, thought, knowledge or understanding – an impenetrable cultural trope (Shoesmith, 2016, p.209) providing, I argue, 'cover' for the transgressions of other agencies.

This habitual blaming impacts on children. It has produced a culture of fear among social workers and their leaders, which is heightened after a case of familial homicide. Fear drives a sharp increase in the number of children being brought into the care system (Cafcass, 2008/9; Shoesmith, 2016). As a result, since 2008 the number of children in the care of local authorities in the UK has doubled to over 100,000 children but with no reduction in familial child homicide (NSPCC Learning, 2021, 2024). Such numbers not only create pressures on finding enough foster and adoptive families but also break up mainly poor families, bringing into care children who in a different context would never have been there.

2. The case of Baby P

The case of Baby P, whilst to some degree an outlier, does bring the context of leading children's services into sharp focus. Peter died in 2007. His mother, her boyfriend and his brother were convicted of 'causing or allowing' his death. I was the DCS in the London Borough of Haringey where he died. Peter was one of 250 children 'at risk' known to social workers in my department. Twenty days after the convictions, the Labour Government's Secretary of State, Ed Balls, sacked me from my statutory role as DCS on live TV, and four social workers followed a few months later, after Ed Balls directed Haringey to 'consider staffing issues arising from the Peter Connelly case' (Employment Tribunal 3302495/2009, paragraph 15.31). By 2011, I had won my case in London's High Court of Appeal against Balls and my employer (*R (Shoesmith) v Ofsted and Others, 2011*), but my career, and those of the social workers, had come to a sudden end.

With a focus on leadership, it's important to outline that in 2001 I was Haringey's deputy director of education, having been one of Her Majesty's Inspectors of Schools (HMI). Ofsted (2002) found the quality of leadership of the senior officers in the Education Department to be 'good'.

By 2003 I had been appointed as director of education, and Ofsted (2003) commented on the 'vision, drive and energy shown by the director'. Two years later I became DCS under the Children Act (2004), which brought Education and Children's Social Care together. Ofsted (2006) judged my leadership to be 'strong and dynamic…supported by many examples of good leadership at all levels'.

A further 11 themed inspections all had positive outcomes between 2006 and 2008 but, in the days after the convictions of those responsible for Baby P's death, Balls ordered another Ofsted inspection which claimed that there was, 'insufficient leadership and management…from senior officers' (Ofsted, 2008). Balls used the report to sack me, referring to me on live TV as 'not fit for office', a comment judged in court to be without foundation (High Court Judgement, The Royal Courts of Justice, 23 April 2010, paras. 302–303).

Understanding these dramatic changes in judging leadership is best discussed in four sections, each drawing upon the context of leading children's services.

The first section concerns the lack of knowledge among the UK population about the realities of harm to children. There is little to no awareness among the public, or indeed politicians, of the high incidence of familial child homicide which, for over 50 years, has claimed the lives of on average one child every week. After Peter's death, I was asked on live radio if I could guarantee that no more children would become victims. I answered, 'No one can give you that guarantee, and I think that's something we must be honest about.' But this was the 'wrong' answer; I was accused of being 'callously disdainful as well as absurd' (Shoesmith, 2016, pp.133–134). Labour Prime Minister Gordon Brown (and others) gave the 'right' answer when he pledged that he would make sure it never happened again. But since Peter died, unknown to the public, and perhaps also to Brown, over 70 further children had already become victims.

The second section considers the responses of each child protection agency to Peter's death. Haringey Council focused on a thorough, well-documented and transparent account of social workers' contact with Peter and planned for a media briefing. Social workers were subjected to a disciplinary process which found no evidence of gross misconduct, a finding later upheld by their own professional body.

At the media briefing following the convictions, our position that no social worker would be sacked inflamed the journalists who instead demanded my resignation. Someone had to be blamed. My sense of being an upright, honest and experienced professional took seconds to trash. I recalled that I had declined advice from a long-standing leader of children's social services that sacking the social workers, despite the lack of evidence, was the 'only way to survive yourself', reinforcing the embeddedness of blaming social workers.

That evening, the head of Haringey's human resources complimented me on my broadcast media interview and the chief executive thanked me by taking me out to dinner. It would never have occurred to me (or possibly to them) that in less than three weeks they would preside over my sacking and within the year they would testify against me in court (High Court Judgement para. 113).

Following a child death or a serious injury to a child, and in line with government policy, an independent Serious Case Review (SCR) was published after those responsible for Peter's death were convicted. Each child protection agency contributed to the SCR with an outline of their contact with the child. The SCR set out recommendations for Haringey's social workers, health professionals from the primary care trust, the world-famous Great Ormond Street Hospital (GOSH) and London's Metropolitan police officers.

Whilst outrageous lies raged about social workers, the case of the health professionals and police had little public attention. Issues with the conduct of Peter's family doctor and the GOSH community clinic were never brought fully to public attention. A GOSH locum paediatrician saw Peter four months after he was referred by the social worker and two days before his death (Dyer, 2011). It transpired that she was not qualified to 'stand in' (Sibert and Hodes, 2008)[1] for that clinic. But GOSH alongside the tabloid media turned its ire on the doctor and avoided serious negative media attention and/or any lasting loss of reputation.

The Metropolitan Police too had serious issues with their conduct in Peter's case. The day before Peter died, they met his mother and told her, after two previous arrests, that they had no case against her. It transpired

---

[1] This information is in the report commissioned by GOSH from Professor Sibert and Dr Hodes – the full report (known as the Sibert Report) was published on the GOSH website around 2011 after lobbying from a whistleblower.

that the case had had no investigating officer for almost three months and on the day that Peter died police had no evidence to draw upon. To defend themselves they embarked on an outrageous campaign of avoiding blame and protecting their reputation by publicly attacking social workers and deflecting attention. The police's culpability and shortcomings only emerged years later with the publication of a second SCR which drew upon two internal police reports and an unpublished report from Her Majesty's Inspectorate of Constabulary. The latter contained criticisms which were never included in the published Ofsted report (2008) used to sack me.[2]

The direct criticisms that the police made of social workers in broadcast interviews and published in *The Sun* were shown by the publication of the full report of the second SCR to be entirely false (Haringey Local Safeguarding Children Board, 2010). For example, HMIC is critical of police conduct after the referral on 1 June (Shoesmith 2016, p 202) but police claimed in the media that they had 'suggested three times that the baby should be taken into care and sought legal advice, but social workers sent him back to his mother' (*Evening Standard* 11/11/08 and Shoesmith, 2016, p.139). The SCR2 full report is clear that the MPS had put Peter's case to the Crown Prosecution Service (CPS) on 31 July but was advised 'no further action' as evidence of non-accidental injury was not confirmed in relation to the arrests in December or June, and there was no evidence of a perpetrator (Department for Education, 2008).

For example, HMIC is critical of police conduct after the referral on 1 June 2007, but police claimed in the media that they had begged social workers to take Peter into care.

Haringey Council, police, GOSH, Ofsted and the chair appointed by Balls who sat at the table for the second SCR, I argue, must have borne witness to evidence that would have made a material difference to those social workers, the paediatrician and myself who were so publicly sacked. But by then, the media had moved on and it appeared that these senior people protected their and each other's reputations.

The third section tackles the interdependence between party politics and sections of the print and broadcast media which unashamedly exploited Peter's death. The leader of the opposition, David Cameron, in his ambition

---

2   The full report of the second SCR, which is usually kept confidential, was published in an act of party politics by the incoming Conservative Government in 2010. At the same time, a confidential report from HMIC was made available by a whistleblower and contained serious criticisms which were never included in the published Ofsted report (2008) used to sack me (Shoesmith, 2016).

to become prime minister, attacked the Labour Government of 11 years and especially Balls' Children's Department and its Children Act (2004).

Cameron teamed up with Rupert Murdoch, head of News International, and employed Murdoch's former editor Andy Coulson, newly released from prison for phone-hacking, as his communications director. Coulson had had a personal relationship with Rebekah Brooks, editor of *The Sun* tabloid newspaper. Together, it seemed that the trio had a story to support Cameron into government, intimidate Balls and sell newspapers.

As public opprobrium rose to shocking heights, with 1.4 million people alleged to have signed *The Sun*'s petition to have me and the social workers sacked, could Balls have told the public that 57 other children had been victims of familial child homicide in the same year as Peter and expected to survive in his job? Probably not.

Instead, having put out a neutral press statement (Shoesmith, 2016, pp.136–137) Balls seemed forced to join the opposition in his attack on myself and Haringey social workers (pp.142–143); I think he joined the tabloid media and the public anger and used the Ofsted report to sack me and save himself. The narrative that social workers and I were responsible for Peter's death had become firmly embedded as a punitive populist news story subjected to post-truth and false news. Politicians had chosen to engage in 'moral rhetoric' and 'emotional politics' (Warner, 2015, p.113) which created hostilities against social workers.

The opportunity for politicians to engage in relational leadership, which might have enabled the public to mourn the death of a child and to learn something about familial child homicide and the work of social workers, was not only lost but also seemed to be beyond their capability (Shoesmith, 2016, p.202).

The fourth and final section is the 2008 Ofsted inspection commissioned by Balls. The public outcry, whilst orchestrated by Balls and others, had become the problem he needed to solve.

Emails released to the High Court showed that Balls' department asked the head of Ofsted to ensure that the report provided 'definitive evidence on which the Minister can act'. Given the published report, it would appear that she complied (High Court Judgement, The Royal Courts of Justice, 23 April 2010, para. 224).

Emails attached to 16 drafts of the Ofsted report revealed that most of the people involved in writing the final report had not been part of the inspection team that had come to Haringey. Those who had made repeated objections to the false negative findings being inserted were ignored. One

Ofsted inspector who had been part of the team advised the lead inspector that they did not have the evidence to support the paragraph on leadership and management (MR email on 28 November 2008 at 01.04), and minutes before I was so dramatically sacked asked if it was too late to make amendments (MR email on 1 December 2008 at 13.53).

The High Court Judges commented that Haringey Council 'might not have been quite so confident in their decision...to dismiss [me and others]... had they known the problems with the inspection and the process by which the final report assumed the form it did' (High Court Judgement, The Royal Courts of Justice, 23 April 2010, para. 50).

The Leveson Inquiry (2012) into the culture, practice and ethics of the media provided startling evidence of just how concerned Balls was about his own position. Brooks, editor of *The Sun*, had rung Balls a few days before I was sacked but denied that she had ordered Balls to sack me. Nick Davies, however, in his book *Hack Attack* (2014, p.223), claimed that a government official was listening to that call and reported that Brooks was blunt and threatening, telling Balls to sack me as 'we don't want to turn this thing [the petition] on you'.

The tragic death of Baby P had become a complex multi-layered, dynamic and fast-moving process of blame avoidance, protecting reputations, false accusations, cover-up, untruths, denial and a series of investments and dependencies between many senior professional people and politicians, which many will have known was untrue.

They each hid behind the other. The story raises interesting and challenging questions about a culture which forces organizations to first and foremost protect their reputations and prevent their transgressions from being made public, at such a high cost to others. It is a culture which is increasingly focused on naming, shaming and blaming, with headlines written to sell newspapers at the expense of truth or understanding.

This is the context in which DCSs lead. It is how 'our society' deals with familial child homicide.

3. The implications for the leadership of children's social care

Changing the cultural trope that blames social workers will take time and careful strategic planning across the whole profession. Above all, I argue that the social work profession must look to itself to change this narrative. No one else can do it. I suggest a four-fold focus.

The first focus or step is to establish a positive presence in public life. In effect, apply your skills in relational leadership to the public, especially politicians, to educate them about your work. Perhaps a column in a local newspaper, 'A day in the life of a social worker', which discusses successes and failures and the hard choices you must often make. Outline how things can go so badly wrong in a family, how domestic abuse that might affect the mother can also affect children and how social workers can help. Give reassurances that seeking help does not mean you 'lose' your children. Raise public awareness about familial child homicide, its frequency and its consequences. The 'social work voice' is strong in the 'trade press' such as *Community Care* but must 'break through' into mainstream media on a regular basis. Engage with broadcast media positively and actively challenge dramatized stereotypes.

Second, give details about resourcing – what is it, where does it come from, where is it spent, could it be spent to achieve better outcomes? What are caseloads? How might greater resourcing be spent, and what might the outcomes be? What form of investment, not only financial but also better support of social workers, might reduce the number of children in care?

Third, in the multi-agency context, with its power imbalances and conflicting perceptions, build social work confidence and resilience, and demonstrate and contribute specific and unique social care skills and knowledge. Challenge others with evidence, and do not be pushed aside from your professional view – even though occasionally it might be wrong.

Fourth, develop a new discourse, the one the late Professor Andrew Cooper told us we lack when children die in dreadful circumstances. It is only DCSs and their teams who can tackle this. Social workers are not (usually) responsible for familial child homicide, but how can this be conveyed? Engage with the emotions it brings to the fore for social workers and the public. Identify a person(s) who has the relational skills and the gravitas to speak up in public, to explain the function of the need to blame and offer a new perspective. The detail of a case is not important; social workers have a right to a fair hearing. Create networks as a profession to support colleagues struggling to cope with aggressive public responses.

Overall, mobilize the nation's 100,000 social workers. Consider how resilience and courage, reflection and learning, pride and reward, truth and transparency can be built into everyday social work experience. Raise the profession's self-esteem and extend your relational leadership skills to challenge and ultimately change the culture. Set out a ten-year plan to achieve it.

REFLECTIONS

1. How can my experience, reflected in this chapter, help to shift the 'impenetrable cultural trope' of simply blaming social workers?
2. To what extent are mediated politics and the 'whipping up' of public opprobrium driving decisions and responses of senior leaders?
3. How can senior leaders drive a realistic discussion about the limits of social care services in protecting children?

References

Cafcass (2008/9) Annual Reports and Accounts since 2008/9. www.cafcass.gov.uk

Cooper, A. (2010) 'Social Work Now – The State of Mind We're In.' Unpublished document. London: The Tavistock Institute of Human Relations.

Cooper, A. (2014) 'A short psychosocial history of British child abuse and protection: Case studies of mourning in the public sphere.' *Journal of Social Work Practice* 8, 3, 271–285.

Davies, N. (2014) *Hack Attack: How the Truth Caught Up with Rupert Murdoch*. London: Chatto and Windus.

Department for Education (2008). Independent report: Haringey serious case reviews: child A. https://www.gov.uk/government/publications/haringey-local-safeguarding-children-board-first-serious-case-review-child-a

Dyer, C. (2011) 'Great Ormond Street and Baby P: Was there a cover up?' *BMJ 343*, 286–291.

Haringey Local Safeguarding Children Board (2010) *Serious Case Review 'Child A': March 2009*. London: Department for Education. https://assets.publishing.service.gov.uk/media/5a8155a4e5274a2e8ab536d2/second_serious_case_overview_report_relating_to_peter_connelly_dated_march_2009.pdf

Haworth, S., Millar, R. and Schaub, J. (2018) *Leadership in Social Work*. Birmingham: University of Birmingham.

Jones, R. (2014) *The Story of Baby P: Setting the Record Straight*. Bristol: Policy Press.

Laming, H. (2009) *The Protection of Children in England*. London: The Stationery Office.

Leedham, M. (2022) 'Social workers failed to heed warnings: A text-based study of how a profession is portrayed in UK newspapers.' *The British Journal of Social Work 52*, 2, 1110–1128.

Leveson, B. (2012) *An Inquiry into the Culture, Practices and Ethics of the Press*. London: The Stationery Office.

Munro, E. (2011) *The Munro Review of Child Protection*. London: Department for Education.
NSPCC Learning (2021) Statistics briefing: child deaths due to abuse or neglect. https://learning.nspcc.org.uk/media/1652/statistics-briefing-child-deaths-abuse-neglect.pdf
NSPCC Learning (2024) Children in care: statistics briefing. https://learning.nspcc.org.uk/research-resources/statistics-briefings/children-in-care
Ofsted (2002) Inspection of Haringey LEA. https://files.ofsted.gov.uk/v1/file/50002233
Ofsted (2003) Inspection Report Haringey. https://files.ofsted.gov.uk/v1/file/50002221
Ofsted (2006) Haringey Joint Area Review. https://files.ofsted.gov.uk/v1/file/50002230
Ofsted (2008) Haringey Joint Area Review. https://files.ofsted.gov.uk/v1/file/50002229
Ofsted (2015) Joining the Dots: Effective Leadership of Children's Services. https://www.gov.uk/government/publications/effective-leadership-of-childrens-services-joining-the-dots
R (Shoesmith) v Ofsted and Others (2011) EWCA Civ 642, Court of Appeal (Civil Division). www.bailii.org/ew/cases/EWCA/Civ/2011/642.html
Shoesmith, S. (2016) *Learning from Baby P: The Politics of Blame, Fear and Denial*. London: Jessica Kingsley Publishers.
Shoesmith, S. (2023) 'Positive Accountability: From Naming, Shaming and Blaming to Lesson Learning.' In M. Flinders and C. Monaghan (eds) *Questions of Accountability: Prerogatives, Power and Politics*. Oxford: Hart.
Sibert, J. and Hodes, D. (2008) *Review of Child Protection Practice of Dr Sabah Al-Zayyat*. London: Great Ormond Street Hospital NHS Trust.
The Royal Courts of Justice, 23 April 2010. https://www.bailii.org/ew/cases/EWHC/Admin/2010/852.html
Warner, J. (2013) '"Heads Must Roll?" Emotional politics. The press and the death of Baby P.' *British Journal of Social Work 44*, 6, 1637–1653.
Warner, J. (2015) *The Emotional Politics of Social Work and Child Protection*. Bristol: Policy Press.

• Chapter 18 •

NAVIGATE YOUR OWN PATH TO LEADERSHIP

Cedi Frederick

> Dr Cedi Frederick is Chair of North Middlesex University Hospital NHS Trust and has over 40 years of experience across the public, not-for-profit and private sectors. He has held roles for 25 years at a BME (black and minority ethnic) housing association, 12 years at a charity supporting people with disabilities and 5 years at a charity with 2500 staff. Cedi has served as Non-Executive Director on various boards for over 30 years and is owner and Managing Director of Article Consulting.
>
> Cedi is also a former men's international basketball player. He holds an honorary doctorate from Canterbury Christ Church University and has been recognized multiple times as one of Britain's most influential Black people.

My personal journey to leadership started before I was born

It started with the decision taken by my parents, along with many others, to leave the small island paradise of Grenada in 1955 after it had been decimated by Hurricane Janet, a hurricane that claimed over 1000 lives across the Caribbean through to Mexico.

My father never told us why they came to England rather than going to America or Canada, like many other young Grenadians after Hurricane Janet, but that decision led to them becoming part of the now-revered

Windrush generation and me becoming a Son of Windrush. My father came to England on his own in 1955 and found a lodging room in a shared house in South London, with an outside shared toilet. And yes, at that time, there were indeed signs in windows making it very clear to anyone passing by that 'No blacks, no Irish, no dogs' were welcome in many lodging houses! After my father settled in, my mother travelled to London six months later to join him and I was born in 1957. I spent the first few years of my life with my parents in a single room – and then, when the man who had the room across the hallway moved out and my parents took his room, two rooms in a shared house – until my parents had saved enough to buy their first house.

Like many of their generation, and despite all the challenges they faced, including the overt racism on the street, in shops and elsewhere on a day-to-day basis, my parents were grateful that they had been allowed to come to England and genuinely felt that they had come to the motherland. As my father explained to my two siblings and I more than once, he and my mother made a conscious decision upon arriving in England that they were going to do whatever they could to assimilate, contribute and give back to the country that had taken them in, and we should do the same. That, along with raising their three children the right way, would be their legacy.

This may sound cheesy, and perhaps even a little trite, but my father would often say to us, especially on a Sunday afternoon, the one day of the week we children were allowed into the front room as he played his jazz and calypso records on the 'Gram', short for stereogram, a huge piece of furniture that sat under the bay window, 'In life you're measured by what you leave behind.' My father was clear as we were growing up that, in his view, contributing and giving back meant public service, and he was very keen for his children to work in the public sector and for public good. That led to me working and building a 45-year career in the public and not-for-profit sectors, my sister working for the NHS and my brother working in the legal profession.

After arriving in England, my mother soon found a job working for a London local authority as what used to be called an auxiliary (better known now as a healthcare assistant) in a former workhouse opened in 1900, which became a large 'old people's home', which was eventually closed and turned into designer flats. My father resisted the lure of working on the buses or on the railways like many others who came from the Caribbean to London and secured a job working for Cable & Wireless, working nights for 15 years even though he hated it; it paid more than the day shift and more than he could earn working on the London transport network.

When I was old enough, my mother pulled a few strings and got me my first Saturday job (unpaid as I recall) at her 'old people's home', going from floor to floor, pushing a trolley, and selling newspapers and chocolates to the residents. This was about me making a contribution to, serving and respecting older people, many of whom had survived the Second World War. When the local authority closed the care home and replaced it with smaller care homes in the community, my mother transferred to one of these. Through sheer hard work, and following several unsuccessful applications, she secured a series of promotions, and in the last few of her 30+ years spent working for that local authority, she retired as the registered manager of one of those care homes. Growing up, my siblings and I would spend many hours in the care homes my mother worked in and then managed. We would read to residents, sit and talk with them and just be around. I learnt so much from those older people.

Looking back, I can now see how my parents' values of hard work, compassion, respect and service to others, along with their resilience and at times naïve optimism, made me, shaped me and have been the foundation on which I have built my leadership philosophy.

Leadership in sport

From a very early age, I was always good at sport. I was a 200m and 400m runner, cricketer and footballer and played badminton at junior county level. Then one day, soon after a new PE teacher joined my school, I was introduced to the sport of basketball, and my whole world changed. I fell in love with the game and gradually focused all my time on developing my game, which led to a bit of a falling out with my father, as coming from the Caribbean, he'd hoped that I'd commit to becoming a cricketer and playing for Surrey. It soon became clear that I had a talent (and the height) to become a pretty good basketball player, and from the age of 15, it was the only sport I wanted to play. I joined a club that played in the National Basketball League, and I soon found myself playing not only for the under-18 junior team but also the men's team. This was the start of a 17+ year playing career, where I was able to achieve my sporting ambitions of being on a team that won the national championship and representing England at senior men's level.

Playing on a men's team as an impressionable and frankly immature youngster gave me the opportunity to see and feel what was meant by leadership. Colin was the captain of the senior men's team. He had the respect of everyone, not just in the team but right across the club. He had a very calm demeanour, but when he spoke, you listened! He set high standards and made his expectations of himself and every member of the team crystal clear at practice and during games. Playing against grown men as a skinny 17-year-old, I was also able to see how my personal values could be the foundation of my future success. I was never the best or strongest player on that team, but I vowed that no one would ever work harder than me and I would be prepared to sacrifice everything for the benefit of the team.

For those who are not familiar with the game, basketball is the ultimate team sport, and the structure of the game and its philosophy provides the perfect platform on which to build leaders. Within a team, you have positions based on your strengths and clear roles. Five players start the game, and five players can be substituted in and out throughout the game. During any game, if one player has what we call 'a hot hand' and is scoring at will, the other players will sacrifice their own scoring to keep giving him or her the ball. A player with a hot hand may be different from game to game depending on the opposition, so within the team, you soon learn about the principle of leading from the front and leading from behind depending on the situation the team finds itself in.

In my 30s, when my playing career was over, I turned to coaching, from juniors through to professional men's teams. This without doubt was where I learnt my most important leadership lessons – how to achieve results through others. I learnt that to be successful as a coach I needed to:

- be able to paint pictures with words and give players a sense of what team success looked like, how it could be achieved and what their individual contribution needed to be to achieve the shared goal

- be authentic. There is something about great coaches that makes their team believe in them, whether it's as individuals or as a group, and connect with them

- create environments where players motivated themselves. As a coach, I learnt that I could motivate a player and/or the team in the moment, such as in a timeout or a rousing pre-game speech, but for the team to be successful over a long season, a player's motivation needed to come from within, and my job was to create an environment where players motivated themselves – many needed a reason to release their motivation, and it was my job to help them find what I called 'The On Switch'

- invite challenge, invite feedback and listen. I learnt that to be a successful coach, I had to create a culture where players challenged and supported each other and themselves, and how constructive challenge enabled individual and collective growth

- be passionate! I learnt that my passion could be infectious. Not everyone on the team would catch it, but if enough players did, then together we could achieve great things

- provide opportunities for each team member to grow. There was no better feeling than seeing my players develop, change and grow

- trust! Demonstrating trust in your players gives them confidence and self-belief, and enables them to achieve more than they maybe thought was possible.

As a coach, I didn't go on the court and play the game. It was my job to establish our playing philosophy, develop a game plan based on the opposition and the conditions, with the support of my assistant coaches, and then put the right players in the best place to be successful on the day, recognizing who had the hot hand, which of course could be different players at different times in the game. Then, during the game, as the coach, my job was to adjust the game plan based on the time, situation and what the opposition were trying to do to negate our strengths. Then, when it got to crunch time, as the coach, the team looked to me to assess the risks and then make the big calls that would help us win the game. Maybe for coach, I read CEO.

Over time, and much to my surprise, I found that my growing experience and success as a coach was helping me become a better leader in the workplace and, as I have found out since, enabled me to build a personal leadership philosophy and a personal brand that I now know is called 'Servant Leadership': a style that is based on empathy, listening, stewardship and commitment to the personal growth of others.

Being a black leader

I can't write about my personal journey to leadership without talking about my experience as a black man leading in what is fundamentally a white corporate world. I decided early in my career that if I was going to be successful, I would have to put myself in situations that I would find challenging and scary. I would have to learn to deal with rejection and disappointment and, not for the first time, my father's wise words shared on a Sunday afternoon that I didn't understand at the time started to make sense. He would say to us again and again, 'Remember, being "as good as" will not be good enough.'

As I unsuccessfully applied for promotions and jobs again and again, I realized that in order to progress in my career, I would have to be clearly and demonstrably better than every other candidate and bring something different into the interview room, a different perspective of leadership.

This prompted me, in my early 30s, to put myself forward to join the board of a small housing association as a non-executive director, as I believed this would give me a taste of what it was like being around the top table. That decision may have been the most important of my career. Not because I was part of a strategic decision-making body, but because a vastly experienced board member with many years of executive leadership experience decided to take me under his wing, support and guide me. He questioned and challenged me; he gave me confidence and self-belief. In those days, it wasn't called coaching and mentoring, but that's what it was, although I didn't recognize it.

Many years later, when we were chatting, I asked him why he gave me so much time and his response was simple. He said, 'Because I could see something in you.' Then, as my career developed, others saw something in me and offered their help and support, which in turn gave me the confidence to reach out to others and ask for advice, and to my continued surprise, no one ever said they were too busy to have a chat, answer a question or offer advice.

This, along with the support of my wife and family who always believed in me, gave me the strength to keep putting myself out there and to keep going for opportunities that would allow me to maximize my contribution as a leader and to do so in ways that were important to me and allowed me to lead in my own authentic way, be that in an executive or non-executive capacity over 30+ years.

Has my journey to leadership been easy? Has it been straightforward? Far from it. I have battled imposter syndrome at every stage of my career. I have constantly questioned myself and my ability to lead. Walking into a room full of white (mostly male) CEOs and looking around and not seeing another face like mine, I've asked myself, 'Am I here, have I been invited only because of the colour of my skin? Am I a token, or have I been invited because they feel I have a meaningful contribution to make?'

Over the years, I have found this pressure wearing, and at times, it has had a corrosive impact on my health. However, it has not stopped me from continuing to challenge myself, even today as I reach the twilight of my career, by putting myself in these uncomfortable situations.

Early in my career, I chose to, as I've described it, 'swallow the bile'. There were so many times when I wanted to scream and shout about the unfair treatment I and many like me received, but every time, as my anger rose inside me, I would swallow it down. My parents were very clear with us growing up that we had to fit in and respect the institutions of the state, and if we challenged 'the System', it would not end well for us. As a result, I was never a campaigner like many others and early in my career I never put my head above the parapet. I have carried high levels of guilt for not speaking out, going on marches or loudly speaking truth to power. But, as my wife and friends constantly remind me, maybe if I had, I wouldn't be where I am today, so I must use my position now to make things better for the current and future generations like me. I do that by coaching and mentoring others and advocating for, influencing and leading change at every level.

So leadership isn't just about what we do, it's about who we are. It starts with us understanding ourselves and how our histories have shaped us and the lessons we've learnt along the way. I learnt that to be true to myself and to the values within which I was raised, my leadership role lies within public service. My athletic career taught me that the best leaders are agile and have the humility to spot and support the 'hot hand'. And just as I benefited from the forward-thinking leaders who saw potential in me, so I've made a point of paying this forward to others. To be authentic leaders, we have to move in a way that feels true to us, so my approach to overcoming barriers has been to work extra hard to succeed within a system that might otherwise have excluded me. I hope this has gone some way to challenging the assumptions I've faced and to reducing the barriers for others. And I'm heartened to see more black leaders following in my footsteps.

Leadership is hard and it's important to acknowledge our struggles, mistakes and regrets. But I've understood from when I pushed the newspaper trolley that there's work to be done, and after 45 years, I still feel I have the potential to offer more. 'You're measured by what you leave behind.' Don't measure me just yet!

The answer's leadership, now what's the question?

> **REFLECTIONS**
>
> 1. How do you maintain the personal resilience to stay the course on your leadership journey?
> 2. How do you ask for help, be that through a coach and/or a mentor?
> 3. How can you be your authentic self throughout your leadership journey? Because ultimately, we have to look at ourselves in the mirror.

Subject Index

Entries followed by f relate to figures; entries followed by n relate to notes.

absolute equalitarianism 87
Achilles' heel 31
action (narrow focus on) 73–4
adaptive leadership 138–9
adrenaline rush 75
anxiety 'containment' 132
Ardern, Jacinda 8–9
authentic leadership 75–6, 137–41
autopoiesis 39

Baby P (death of Peter Connelly)
    blaming of social workers
        164, 165, 166, 167–9
    demand for Cafcass's
        services after 17–18
    dismissals after 164, 165, 166
    GOSH response 166
    Haringey Council response 165–6
    HMIC report 167, 167n
    Metropolitan Police conduct 166–7
    Ofsted report 167, 168–9
    Serious Case Reviews (SCRs)
        166, 167, 167n
    The Sun's conduct 167–9
Balls, Ed 164, 165, 168, 169
basketball 175–6
being (denial of) 74–5
best-idea-wins principle 83, 87
Bion, Wilfred 132
black leader (being a) 178–9

Brooks, Rebekah 168, 169
Brown, Gordon 165
burnout 51, 57
'busy rescuer' 75
butterfly effects 60–1

Cafcass
    absorbing hostility 16–17
    building the team and culture 14–15
    demand, cost and quality 17–19
    Family Justice Young People's
        Board (FJYPB) 16
    improvement journey 15–16
    learning from early days 12–13
    relative stability 19
    survival mode 13–14
    talent management programme 14
Cameron, David 167–8
Camphill Village Trust 44, 47
Care Act (2014) 35
'care in the community' 53
'care management' (shift from) 35
catalytic probes 36, 38
change
    examining values and 124–5
    is always personal 43–5
    requires intentional effort 123–9
    SCARF model 45
    slash and burn approaches to 40
    working with the flow of 37, 39

change communication
  answering questions 48, 49
  clarity 45–6
  collaboration 46–7
  consistency 47
  reflections about 48–9
  simplifying the messages 48
  see also communication
character strengths 114
checks/counterchecks of decisions 40
child protection *see* Baby P (death of Peter Connelly); directors of children's services (DCSs)
climate change
  emotional responses to 154
  see also environmental sustainability in adult social care
closed systems 38
co-production
  building 120–1
  diverse representation in 121
  equalizing power distribution 128–9
  genuine trust and 126
  lifting others up 123–4
  reimagining care and support 122–3
  respect and dignity 126–8
  and 'the water we swim in' 125–6
  treating people as fellow human beings 121–2
coaching (sports) 176–7
cognitive cultures 77, 78
collaboration
  in change communication 46–7
  see also lateral collaboration; sibling leadership
Colwell, Maria 18
'command and control' culture 23–4, 39
commodification of work 74–5
communication
  empathetic 8–9
  the 'how' of 49
  see also change communication
competition in the workplace 62–3
complex adaptive systems 33–4, 35

complexity
  complex adaptive system (Xshire as) 35
  hot cognition and understanding 133
  new practice model (in Xshire) 35–8
complexity theory 33–4, 37
connectedness
  importance of 7
  with staff 20
consistency 47
Coulson, Andy 168
covert power assertion 86
Covid-19 pandemic
  impact of 110–1
  mistakes after 117
crisis
  lessons learnt during 116–17
  planning for a 111–12
  see also relational leadership in a crisis
culture
  cognitive 77, 78
  emotional 76–8
  fear-driven 23–4

defensive systems 39–40
depersonalization of tasks 40
depression 55
dignity (in co-production) 126–8
dilemmatic spaces 106–7
Diogenes Paradigm 103–6
directors of children's services (DCSs)
  challenging context of children's services 163–4
  implications of current cultural trope 169–71
  statutory role of 164
  see also Baby P (death of Peter Connelly)
disability community (diverse needs within) 120
disappointment
  Alexander at Gordium 106
  Alexander the Great and Diogenes 104–5
  in dilemmatic spaces 106–7

experiences of 102–3
  learning from the 'Diogenes
    Paradigm' 103–6
  practising 103–4
  ring-fencing the 'agora' 106–9
dismissal/sacking
  after case of Baby P 164, 165, 166
  loss of experienced leaders 56
  MacIntyre charity 54
diverse teams 65–6
'doing the doing' 74, 75
Double Helix of Exposure and
    Expansion 26–7, 26f

Ehn, Andreas 83
elevated siblings 98
emergence (in a complex adaptive
    system) 34, 37, 38
emergency preparedness 157–8
emotional culture 76–8
emotional leadership
  Jacinda Ardern 8–9
  see also vulnerability
emotional literacy 148
emotions
  authentic display of 8–9, 75–6
  as information 72–3
  offering opportunity to share 80
  as a 'thing' to manage 73–5
  unregulated 133
empathetic communication 8–9
environmental sustainability
  in adult social care
  emergency preparedness 157–8
  increasing workforce
    capabilities 158–9
  overview 153–4
  practical ideas for leadership 156–9
  recognizing leaders' vulnerabilities
    as strengths 154
  streamlining assessments of need 157
  through prevention 156
  weather-related absenteeism 154
equalitarianism/equality (absolute) 87
equalizing power distribution 128–9

Equity, Diversity and Inclusion
    (EDI) processes 66
ethical literacy 146
Every Child Matters 138, 139
excellence without vulnerability 28–30

familial child homicide statistics 165, 168
Family Justice Young People's
    Board (FJYPB) 16
fast and slow thinking 133
fathers' groups 17
fear of raising concerns 78–9
fear-driven culture 23–4, 79–80
'firefighting' 20
Five Ways to Wellbeing
    framework 55–6
Floyd, George 92
four domains of leadership 113, 113f
future focused literacy 149

geographical relocation 14, 46–7
Gordian knot 106
Growth Loop 27–8, 28f
growth mindset 9

Hansson, Petra 83
Heroic Leader, The 7, 31, 116
hierarchies (traditional) 139
hostility (absorbing) 16–17
hot cognition 133
human (making yourself) 28–30
  see also vulnerability

imposter syndrome 178–9
'influencers' (working with) 16
intentional effort 123–9
interdependency (acceptance of) 89–90
International Centre for
    Child Protection 130

Jobs, Steve 7

knowledge
  domain 145–6
  slowly increasing your 13–14

lateral collaboration
  acceptance of interdependency 89–90
  authority negotiation in 86
  dynamics of 85
  early life models 87–9
  leaders' experiences of 83–5
  navigating 89
  peer leaders 88–9
  role accountability and 85
legal aid budget cuts 18
legal literacy 145
listening to voices of lived experience 15–16
literacies
  aesthetics domain 148–9
  explanation domain 146–8
  knowledge domain 145–6
lived experience (listening to) 15–16
lonely hero model 116

MacIntyre (charity) 53
mental health 55–6
mentoring 178
mobilizing staff 14, 46–7
moral compass (retaining your) 114
Murdoch, Rupert 168

Nadella, Satya 9
network nudges 66–7
night terrors 54, 55
nimble leadership 138–9
norms 61–2
nudges 66–7

obsessive equality 87
omnipotence (idolization of) 31
open systems 38
operational experience 13
operational structure (positioning the work at heart of) 13
orchestral conductor ('sibling') 94
organizational literacy 148

parental alienation 17

peer leaders 88–9
  see also lateral collaboration
personal experiences (drawing upon) 13
political literacy 149
power
  covert assertion of 86
  myth of 31
procedures (focus on) 39
proportionate working 16
prudence 114–15
psychoanalytical understanding 40
psychodynamic literacy 147
public perception of social workers 163–9, 168

qualities (character) 114
questions (answering) 48, 49

racism 174, 178–9
recognition (and wellbeing) 63–4
Reflective Practice Groups 108
reimagining care and support 122–3
relational leadership
  reflections for 19–20
  in Safeguarding Adults Boards 144–9
  values of 139–40
relational leadership in a crisis
  five golden rules 112–13
  keeping your bearings 112–13
  overview 111–12
  prudence 114–15
  ressourcement 115
  self-care 116
relational literacy 147
repetition (rule of seven) 49
resignations
  as immediate reaction to serious concern 57
  loss of experienced leaders 56
  MacIntyre (charity) 53
  Winterbourne View Joint Improvement Programme 54
respect (in co-production) 126–8
ressourcement 115
right person (importance of getting) 15

'risk' (as socially defined construct) 131
risk assessment
    difficulty of 130–1
    relationship-based practice and 131–2
ritual task performance 40
rule of seven (repetition) 49

safe to fail experiments 36, 38
Safeguarding Adults Boards
    leadership learning points 149–50
    overview 143–5
    relational leadership in 144–9
    see also literacies
safeguarding literacy 146
SCARF model of change 45
self-care *see* support/self-care
self-discipline 140
Servant Leadership 177
Sibert Report 166n
sibling leadership
    elevated siblings 98
    in a paediatrics department 95–6
    sibling matrix 93
    'sibling' orchestral conductor 94
    sibling rivalry/competition 96–7
significance of work (importance of understanding) 18
social comparison 63
social distance 67
social norms 61–2
social workers
    blamed after case of Baby P 164, 165, 166
    public perception of 163–9, 168
soft power 60–1
speaking truth to power 105, 179
sports leadership 175–7
Spotify 83
staff (connection with) 20
stagecraft (campaigners') 17
superheroes 31
supervision 132–5
support/self-care 18, 116
symbolic recognition 64

systemic literacy 147

talent management programme 14
Tesco Clubcard 34
Thakkar, Sara 44
tick-box assessment forms (removal of) 40–1, 122
trust 126
truth-telling 105, 179

Ubuntu 120

values
    common cause in shared 139
    no change without examining 124–5
    in relational leadership 139–40
values literacy 148–9
vulnerability
    at home vs. at work 24–5
    authentic display of 8–9, 75–6
    currency of 26–31
    Double Helix of Exposure and Expansion 26–7, 26f
    and emotionally exposed leadership 23–4
    excellence without 28–30
    Growth Loop 27–8, 28f
    inevitability of 25
    leading through (case example) 30–1
    myth of power and 31
    perceived as weakness 8
    recognizing as strength 154–6

weather-related absenteeism 154
wellbeing
    recognition and 63–4
    see also burnout; mental health; support/self-care
Windrush generation 119, 174–5
Winnicott, Clare 132
Winnicott, Donald 132
Winterbourne View Joint Improvement Programme 52, 54
'wrapping around' a problem 14

Author Index

Academy for Sustainable Innovation 155
Adlam, J. 103, 108
Agass, D. 148, 150
Aked, J. 55
Aknin, L. B. 64
Audit Commission 144

Barlow, J. 130, 152
Barrett, K. C. 72
Behavioural Insights Team 66, 67
Bergsen, A. M. 154
Boahen, G. 154
Boehm, C. 92
Bovey, W. H. 40
Braye, S. 143, 144
Brown, D. 93
Browne, V. 156
Brunori, L. 93

Cafcass 164
Cambridge, P. 149
Charness, G. 67
CIPFA 144
Cocker, C. 146
Coombs, W. T. 111
Cooper, A. 146, 163
Cronen, V. 145

Danely, J. 156
Davies, N. 169
Department for Education 167

Department for Environment, Food and Rural Affairs 154
Department of Health and Social Care 35, 143, 144, 145, 156, 157
Deseret News 23
Donne, J. 101
Dorsey, S. 131
Duffy, S. 38
Dunn, E. W. 64
Dyer, C. 166

Ferguson, H. 131, 132
Forrester, D. 132
Freud, S. 80

Galinsky, A. D. 65
Gallus, J. 64
Ginzberg, R. 93
Gneezy, U. 67
Grant, A. M. 64
Grint, K. 146, 150

Hackett, R. D. 114
Hallsworth, M. 61
Harari, Y. 99
Haringey Local Safeguarding Children Board 167
Haworth, S. 163
Health Foundation, The 34
Hede, A. 40
HM Treasury 138
Hodes, D. 166

AUTHOR INDEX

Holladay, S. 111
Honig, B. 106

Johnson, S. 101
Jones, R. 163, 164
Joubert, S. 113

Kamavarapu, Y. S. 52
Keizer, K. 62
Keltner, D. 72
Kim, S.-J. 111
Kings Fund, The 156
Kreeger, L. 98

Labourdette, M. 114
Laming, H. 163
Lang, P. 145, 148
Larchet, J.-C. 111
Lawrance, E. 153
Leedham, M. 163
Leveson, B. 169
Levin, B. 83
Lindenberg, S. 62
Little, M. 145
Lopez, S. O. 155
Lount, R. B. 65

McManus, J. 111, 116
Mannix, E. 65
Marker, A. 111
Marx, K. 74
Mason, B. 146
Mason, K. 146
Megele, C. 132, 152
Mell, J. N. 65
Menzies, I. E. P. 40
Millar, R. 163
Miller, S. 98
Minor, N. W. 152
Mirzoeff, S. 134
Moore, T. 37
Morris, M. W. 72
Mortlock, J. 158
Munro, E. 39, 163
Murowe, T. 158

Neale, M. A. 65
Nelson-Goens, G. C. 72
Newstead, T. 114
NHS England 38
Nolan Committee on Standards in Public Life 144
Norton, M. I. 64
NSPCC Learning 164

Obholzer, A. 98
O'Flaherty, S. 64
Ofsted 163, 165, 167
OPM 144
Orr, D. 144
Oswald, T. 153

Parker, V. 91, 93
Parmenter, D. 30
Petriglieri, G. 92, 99
Phillips, K. W. 65
Pine, G. 114
pool 112
Poole, E. 112
Pratt, M. 143, 145
Preston-Shoot, M. 142, 143, 144, 145, 146, 148, 149, 150

Rock, D. 45
Rosenow, D. 156
Royal Courts of Justice 165, 168, 169

Sanders, M. T. 64
Scanlon, C. 103, 108
Schaub, J. 163
Shapiro, E. L. 93
Shoesmith, S. 163, 164, 165, 167, 168
Sibert, J. 166
Siegal, D. 72
Skills for Care 153
Smallwood, J. 113
Snowden, D. J. 36, 37, 39
Steg, L. 62
Sutton, J. 38

Tian, T. Y. 65

United Kingdom Parliament 111

Vada, Ø. 34
Van Knippenberg, D. 65
Vercammen, A. 153

Wang, G. 114
Warner, J. 163, 168
Weber, M. 72
Weintrobe, S. 154
Whillans, A. 64

Wiggins, L. 113
Wiles, F. 154
Wilke, G. 97
Wilkins, D. 132
Wilson, S. 114
Woodruff, T. K. 65
Wu, Y. L. 111

Yang, Y. 65
Young, S. 154
Yu, N. 149

RAISING READERS
Books Build Bright Futures

Dear Reader,

We'd love your attention for one more page to tell you about the crisis in children's reading, and what we can all do.

Studies have shown that reading for fun is the **single biggest predictor of a child's future life chances** – more than family circumstance, parents' educational background or income. It improves academic results, mental health, wealth, communication skills, ambition and happiness.[1]

The number of children reading for fun is in rapid decline. Young people have a lot of competition for their time. In 2024, 1 in 10 children and young people in the UK aged 5 to 18 did not own a single book at home.[2]

Hachette works extensively with schools, libraries and literacy charities, but here are some ways we can all raise more readers:

- Reading to children for just 10 minutes a day makes a difference
- Don't give up if children aren't regular readers – there will be books for them!
- Visit bookshops and libraries to get recommendations
- Encourage them to listen to audiobooks
- Support school libraries
- Give books as gifts

There's a lot more information about how to encourage children to read on our website: **www.RaisingReaders.co.uk**

Thank you for reading.

hachette UK

---

1. OECD, '21st-Century Readers: Developing Literacy Skills in a Digital World', 2021, https://www.oecd.org/en/publications/21st-century-readers_a83d84cb-en.html
2. National Literacy Trust, 'Book Ownership in 2024', November 2024, https://literacytrust.org.uk/research-services/research-reports/book-ownership-in-2024